SEO FITNESS WORKBOOK:
The Seven Steps to Search Engine Optimization Success on Google

2016 EDITION

BY JASON MCDONALD, PH.D.

© 2016, JM INTERNET GROUP

https://www.jm-seo.org/

Tel. 800-298-4065

Contents

0.1	**Introduction**	Pg.	2
1.1	**Attitude**	Pg.	15
1.2	**Goals**	Pg.	21
1.3	**Basics**	Pg.	27
2.1	**Keywords**	Pg.	33
2.2	**Keyword Worksheet**	Pg.	50
3.1	**Page Tags**	Pg.	61
3.2	**Website Structure**	Pg.	75
3.3	**SEO Audit**	Pg.	87
4.1	**Content SEO**	Pg.	92
4.2	**Press Release SEO**	Pg.	100
4.3	**Blogging**	Pg.	107
5.1	**Link Building**	Pg.	112
5.2	**Social Media SEO**	Pg.	127
5.3	**Local SEO**	Pg.	135
6.1	**Metrics**	Pg.	146
7.1	**Learning**	Pg.	154

0

INTRODUCTION

Welcome to the *SEO Fitness Workbook, 2016 edition*! Fully revised and updated for 2016, this workbook explains how to succeed at *Search Engine Optimization* (*SEO*) in **seven steps**. SEO, of course, is the art and science of **getting your company** to show at the **top** of relevant Google or Bing searches, for **free**. With most customers turning first to Google, Bing, or other search engines, SEO is your free gateway to more inquiries, more customers, and more sales.

SEO =

FREE ADVERTISING ON GOOGLE

Free advertising on Google? Yippie! On Bing? Double Yippie! But, here's the rub: **SEO seems really complicated**. Is it "too good to be true?"

Believe me, I understand your frustration with SEO and with the frauds, scoundrels, and dishonest robbers who plague my beloved SEO industry. I know the complaints, and I hear them often in my classes in the San Francisco Bay Area, including my very popular "Marketing without Money" class at Stanford Continuing Studies. Here are some of the most **common complaints**:

- We need to get our company to the top of Google for relevant keywords; our competitors are there, but we're not!
- Our website sucks. It not only looks terrible, we don't even show for our own company name!
- We hired an SEO company, spent several thousands of dollars, and achieved nothing. So-called "SEO experts" are just thieves!

- I don't understand computers, can't write HTML, and I can't do SEO. Help!
- I pay attention to Google, and SEO seems to change constantly: there's no way we can keep up: Penguin, Panda, Hummingbird. Isn't there a nice animal in the Google zoo?
- We hired an obscure third world SEO firm, they built 50,000 blog links, and now we have been obliterated by Google's Penguin update.
- SEO is just too hard for anyone without a degree in Computer Science from Yale University to be able to do. We give up! (They then start uncontrollably sobbing).
- We'll just do AdWords (and spend thousands of dollars). Google clearly needs more money from struggling small businesses just like ours, so they can invest in drones and self-driving cars!

I hear and feel your pain. I am just a regular guy, and I have been confronted with what I call **techtimidation** probably as much as you have.

Techtimidation =

The use of jargon by techies to intimidate mere mortals

However, I firmly believe that a little education, a lot of hard work, and some common sense are all you really need to succeed in SEO. The computer nerds (and Googlers) would like us all to believe SEO is difficult – no impossible – without a computer science degree.

Poppycock. Hokum. Hooey. Malarkey, Rubbish, Baloney and even B.S.!

You can do SEO. You can succeed at it. It is easier than you think.

The purpose of this book is to, **first**, make you believe in yourself, **second**, empower you with the basic knowledge of how the SEO game is played, and **third**, to help you make a detailed SEO plan for your business.

More on this later.

Let's return to SEO, *the art and science of getting your product, service or company to the top of Google and Bing.*

Google Algorithm Updates

Recent years have seen some terrifying Google search engine algorithm updates, namely *Penguin* and *Panda*. In a nutshell, *Penguin* has been an algorithm attack against "low quality" links, and *Panda* has been an algorithm attack against poor quality content. In addition, Google has recently penalized sites that are not "mobile friendly" and made major changes to local search results. Its Hummingbird update was a move towards "semantic search." Google, in short, has been busy changing the rules of the SEO game.

Google makes changes, and we have to adapt. But here's the good news: the **basics** haven't really changed, and if you stick to the **basics** according to "white hat" SEO – you'll be fine.

Let me repeat that:

the basics have not changed in SEO.

This workbook will explain what not to do, and what to do, to succeed at SEO in this post-*Penguin*, post-*Panda* world. And, it will also educate you on the unchanged basic rules of SEO success.

(If you don't know what *Panda* and *Penguin* are… don't worry – I'll explain later).

Back to SEO.

What is SEO? SEO, of course, is the art and science of getting your company, product, or service to the top of Google's organic (free) results. If you're a seller of "industrial fans," it means when customers search for "industrial fans," they see your company's product at the top of Google.

Why is SEO so valuable? Simply put, SEO is valuable because SEO is **free** advertising on Google! And there ain't nothing better than free, is there? (Well, a few things, but please return to the subject at hand).

Customers turn to Google first to find new products and services, new companies and consultants. And showing up for "free" means you are getting free advertising.

Everybody uses Google!

(*Well, a few people use Bing, but the game is the same. Rest assured that all techniques covered in this Workbook apply equally to Bing*).

An SEO Checkup

Some questions for you:

1. Do your potential customers use Google or Bing to find companies, products or services like yours?
2. Taking a common search query relevant to your company (e.g., "industrial fans," or "best pizza Tulsa"), do you see your company on Page 1, positions 1, 2, or 3? High on the page, or low on the page?
3. Taking a whole bunch of keyword search queries (*the "universe" of search terms by which customers might search for your company, product or service*), do you generally show up on Page 1 of Google, positions 1-3? positions 1-10?, or not at all?

If you generally appear on Page 1, positions 1, 2, or 3, for all your relevant keywords, you can stop reading this book. You pass with an A+. If you generally do not appear, then keep reading. You need help.

If you have no idea what search word "queries," "positions" on Google, or "high" vs. "low" on the page mean, don't worry. Don't feel stupid. You need help, and I am going to teach you.

Isn't SEO Hard?

Well, that's what Google would like you to think (*so spend money on AdWords...*) And that's what many in the SEO industry would like you to think (*so pay us big consulting fees, and don't ask any questions!*)

I don't agree. *SEO isn't easy, but it isn't exactly hard either.*

I've taught thousands of people in my online classes, in classes in the San Francisco Bay Area, and in corporate workshops, and I can confirm there is a lot of confusion about SEO. People think it's hard, or impossible, or mysterious, and that's simply not correct.

SEO =
GOOGLE FITNESS

SEO, you see, is a lot like **physical fitness**. Although everyone can conceivably run a marathon, for example, few people make the effort to learn how and even fewer take the disciplined steps necessary to train for and ultimately finish a marathon.

> *Does that make running a marathon easy?*
>
> *No.*
>
> *But does that make running a marathon hard?*
>
> *Not really.*

Like running a marathon, SEO is **conceptually** simple (*exercise a lot, train with discipline, don't give up*) but **practically** hard (*you have to work at it nearly every day*).

And, of course, the Olympic champions don't just work *hard*, they work *smart*.

That's the beginning of the **good news**. If you just learn how to work smarter (not harder), you'll find that SEO isn't really that hard. And it gets better.

You're Smarter than Your Competitors

In most industries, you'll find that your competitors are not that smart. Most industries are not as competitive in SEO as you would think, and metaphorically speaking, you don't have to run faster than the bear; you just have to run faster than your buddy!

> *Let me rephrase that. You are not competing against Google! You are competing against your competitors, and they aren't that much smarter than you. In fact, I bet they might even be dumber!*

The Seven Steps to SEO Success

This workbook guides you through the **seven steps** to successful SEO. Along the way, we'll set goals, understand technical details, and have fun. Along the way, I will be your "fitness coach" to explain how it all works and to motivate you to keep trying. **You can do this!**

Throughout this workbook, I will share with you other examples of businesses that understand SEO and succeed using the **seven steps**.

The **seven steps to SEO fitness** are built on a philosophy of empowerment. Can you understand SEO? Yes you can! Can you implement SEO? Yes you can! It takes some knowledge, it takes some effort, but yes you can do it.

Before we dive in, allow me to share just a few more points of background.

» MEET THE AUTHOR

Well, first of all, who am I and what makes me an expert? My name is Jason McDonald, and I have been active on the Internet since 1994 (having invented the Internet along with Al Gore). I have been teaching SEO, AdWords, and Social Media since 2009 - online, in San Francisco, at Stanford University Continuing Studies, at workshops, and in corporate trainings. Over 3000 people have taken my paid trainings; over 25,000 my free webinars. I love figuring out how things work, and I love teaching others! SEO is an endeavor that I understand, and I want to empower you to understand it as well.

Learn more about me at https://www.jasonmcdonald.org/ or at my corporate website https://www.jm-seo.org/.

Don't believe I'm good at SEO, Google "Jason McDonald" (*I'm usually in the top three*), Google "SEO Expert San Francisco" (*you'll see me there*), Google "AdWords Expert Witness" (*Yes, I do legal work – there's good money in it, and I have a daughter in college*), or Google "SEO Classes Chicago" (*You'll see the JM Internet Group," my training and consulting company*). You can even Google "Best Books on SEO," and you'll usually see my booklist, with this book at the top. Clever, huh?

Uncle? Give up? Still don't believe me? Call me up, or email me before you buy this book, and I'll give you reference examples of my SEO clients (*who don't want their competitors to know about me*).

» WHY THIS BOOK IS DIFFERENT

There are quite a few books on SEO out there! There are zillions of blog posts! There are thousands of SEO consultants! There are hundreds of crazy harebrained schemes...

But there is only one **workbook**: the *SEO Fitness Workbook*.

How is a *workbook* different from a *book*? Here's how.

First of all, this workbook speaks in **practical, no-nonsense English.** Whereas most of the SEO books out there are *by* experts *for* experts, this workbook explains SEO in plain English and does not get lost in the details. Most businesspeople don't need to know every gory detail about SEO; rather they need practical, hands-on advice about what to do first, second, third and so forth. The *SEO Fitness Workbook* is as much about "doing SEO" as it is about "understanding SEO."

Secondly, the *SEO Fitness Workbook* is **hands-on**. Most SEO books are meant to be passively read. *SEO Fitness Workbook*, by contrast, gives you "hands on" worksheets and deliverables. In fact, each chapter ends with a deliverable marked in red. Each chapter also has TODOS (marked in RED) because a workbook is not just about reading, it's about **doing** and **succeeding**.

Third, while most books are outdated on the day they are published, the SEO Fitness Workbook connects to up-to-date **Internet resources** such as free SEO tools via the companion *SEO Toolbook*, and hands-on YouTube videos that show you how to succeed. After all, in the 21st century, a "how to" book should be more than a book, shouldn't it? It should be a gateway to up-to-date knowledge.

» REGISTER YOUR WORKBOOK FOR FREE ONLINE RESOURCES

Please **register** your *Workbook*. You'll not only get a full-color PDF copy of this *Workbook* to download with active, clickable links to the resources (very handy to read at your computer). You'll also get my *SEO Toolbook*, my secret *SEO Dashboard,* and all the Workbook's companion worksheets to help you step-by-step.

To register, follow these easy steps:

1. Go to https://www.jm-seo.org/workbooks/
2. Click on "SEO Fitness"
3. Enter your passcode: **fitness2016**.
4. If you have any problems, contact me via https://www.jm-seo.org/contact/ or call 800-298-4065 for help.

Sign up for email alerts at https://jm-seo.org/free, and - last but not least- watch a few of my YouTube videos at https://www.youtube.com/jmgrp; you'll find I am as crazy and enthusiastic on video as I am in this book!

▶▶ WHO THIS BOOK IS FOR

I have written *SEO Fitness Workbook* for the following groups of practical business folk:

> **Small Business Owners.** If you own a small business that gets (or could get) significant customer traffic from the Web, this book is for you.
>
> **Small Business Marketers.** If you are in charge of marketing for a small business that gets (or could get) significant customer traffic from the Web, this book is for you.
>
> **Marketing Managers**. If you lead a Web team of inside or outside bloggers, SEO content writers, or other Internet marketing technicians including external SEO companies, this book is for you.
>
> **Web Designers**. If you design websites but want to design sites that not only look good but actually succeed at Google search, this book is for you.
>
> **Non-profit Marketers.** If you work at a non-profit or governmental agency that depends on Web search traffic, then this book is also for you.

Anyone whose organization (and its products, services, or other offerings) would benefit from being at the top of Google, for free, can benefit from the *SEO Fitness Workbook*.

▶▶ THE SEVEN STEPS TO SEO FITNESS

Here are the seven steps to SEO fitness:

1. **Goals**: Define Your Goals
2. **Keywords**: Identify Keywords
3. **On Page SEO:** Get Your Website to "Speak Google"

4. **Content Marketing**: Create Quality Content for Google and for Humans
5. **Off Page SEO**: Build Links, Leverage Social Media, and Go Local
6. **Metrics**: Measure and Learn from Your Results
7. **Learn**: Never Stop Learning!

And here are the seven steps to SEO fitness in more detail:

Step #1: GOALS. SEO, like physical fitness, SEO is purpose-driven! You can't achieve your goals if you don't define what they are.

1.1 Attitude – attitude is everything, and SEO requires a commitment to learning how SEO works as well as a desire to implement positive SEO-friendly changes. Goal 1.1 is to have the right attitude.

1.2 Goals – define what you sell, who your customers are, and how best to reach them. Define website goals such as to get online sales or acquire customer names, phone numbers, and email addresses as sales leads.

1.3 Basics – understand the basics of SEO, i.e. "on page" and "off page" tactics. Goal 1.3 is to understand the SEO game at its most basic level.

Step #2 KEYWORDS – identify your keywords. Keywords drive nearly every aspect of SEO, so you need a well-structured, clearly defined "keyword worksheet."

2.1 Keywords – identify high volume, high value keywords.

2.2 Keyword Worksheet – build a keyword worksheet and measure your rank on Google and Bing.

Step #3 ON PAGE SEO for your website. Once you know your keywords, where do you put them? It begins with page tags, proceeds through website organization, and ends with an "SEO audit" that outlines your SEO strategy. The nerd word for this is "on page" SEO.

3.1 Page Tags – understand basic HTML tags, and weave your target keywords into strategic tags such as the TITLE, META DESCRIPTION, and IMG ALT tags.

3.2 Website Structure – build landing pages, restructure your home page, and optimize website layout through keyword-heavy link sculpting.

3.3 SEO Audit – now that you know the basics of "on page" SEO, conduct an "on page" SEO audit of your website.

Step #4 CONTENT MARKETING. They say that "content is king" in terms of SEO, and they are right. In this section, you'll create a long-term content strategy that moves beyond the "quick fix" of your site to a day-by-day, week-by-week system of SEO-friendly content.

4.1 Content SEO – devise a content strategy, specifically who will do what, when, where, how, and how often – that is, a short and long term SEO content marketing strategy including an inventory of the content you need to succeed.

4.2 Press Release SEO - leverage news and free syndication services for SEO, because press releases are an easy technique to get links and build buzz on social media.

4.3 Blogging – set up a blog that follows best SEO practices, including all-important connections to social media platforms like Google+ and Twitter.

Step #5 OFF PAGE SEO – links and social media. "Off page" SEO leverages external web links and social media to boost your website's authority on Google. Use the traditional tactic of getting relevant inbound links. Then, leverage social media platforms like Twitter, Google+, Facebook, LinkedIn and YouTube to enhance your SEO efforts!

5.1 Link Building – conduct a link building audit and create a long-term link building strategy.

5.2 Social Media SEO – look for social media mention opportunities, and enable relevant social profiles to enhance Google's trust in your website as an authoritative resource.

5.3 Local SEO – local SEO stands at the juncture of SEO, local, and review based marketing, and so we dive into how to optimize a website for local searches.

Step #6 METRICS – measure and learn from your results. Like physical fitness, SEO is a process that starts with a defined set of goals and employs specific measurements about goal achievement.

6.1 Metrics - measure your progress towards the top of Google, inbound keywords, and paths taken by customers once they land on your website.

Step #7 LEARN - never stop learning. SEO starts with self-discovery, proceeds through technical knowledge, and ends with the hard work of implementation.

7.1 Learning – use Chapter 7 to get access to companion **worksheets** and the very important ***SEO Toolbook*** and my ***secret dashboard***, which provide hundreds of free SEO tools, tools to help you in all aspects of SEO, from identifying keywords through page tags to links and social mentions.

» SPREAD THE WORD: WRITE A REVIEW & GET A FREE eBOOK!

If you like the book, please take a moment to write an honest review on Amazon.com. Here's my special offer for those lively enough to write a review –

1. Write your **honest review** on Amazon.com.
2. **Contact** me via https://www.jm-seo.org/contact and let me know your review is up.
3. Include your **email address** and **website URL**, and any quick questions you have about it.
4. I will send you a **free** copy of one of my other such as *AdWords Gotchas*, the *Social Media Workbook*, or my forthcoming *Personal Branding Wor*kbook.

This offer is limited to the first 100 reviewers, and only for reviewers who have purchased a paid copy of the book.

» QUESTIONS AND MORE INFORMATION

I **encourage** my students to ask questions. If you have questions, submit them via https://www.jm-seo.org/contact/. There are two sorts of questions: ones that I know instantly, for which I'll zip you an email answer right away, and ones I do not know instantly, in which case I will investigate and we'll figure out the answer together.

As a teacher, I learn most from my students. So please don't be shy!

- Jason McDonald, Ph.D.

›› COPYRIGHT AND DISCLAIMER

Copyright © 2016, JM Internet Group and Excerpti Communications, Inc., All Rights Reserved. No reproduction or citation without written consent of the publisher. For details and to contact us, visit our website at https://www.jm-seo.org/.

This is a completely **unofficial** guide to SEO. Neither Google nor Bing / Yahoo have endorsed this guide, nor has Google, Bing, or Yahoo nor anyone affiliated with Google, Bing, or Yahoo been involved in the production of this guide.

That's a *good thing*. This guide is **independent**. My aim is to "tell it as I see it," giving you no-nonsense information on how to succeed at SEO.

In addition, please note the following:

- All trademarks are the property of their respective owners. I have no relationship with nor endorsement from the mark holders. Any use of their marks is so I can provide information to you.

- Any reference to or citation of third party products or services whether for Google, Yahoo, Bing, or otherwise, should not be construed as an endorsement of those products or services tools, nor as a warranty as to their effectiveness or compliance with the terms of service of Google, Yahoo, or Bing.

The information used in this guide was derived in October, 2015. However, SEO changes rapidly, so please be aware that scenarios, facts, and conclusions are subject to change without notice.

Additional Disclaimer. Internet marketing is an art, and not a science. Any changes to your Internet marketing strategy, including SEO, Social Media Marketing, and AdWords, is at your own risk. Neither Jason McDonald nor the JM Internet Group nor

Excerpti Communications, Inc. assumes any responsibility for the effect of any changes you may, or may not, make to your website or AdWords advertising based on the information in this guide.

» ACKNOWLEDGEMENTS

No man is an island. I would like to thank my beloved wife, Noelle Decambra, for helping me hand-in-hand as the world's best moderator for our online classes, and as my personal cheerleader in the book industry. Gloria McNabb has done her usual tireless job as first assistant, including updating this edition as well the *SEO Toolbook*. Hannah McDonald and Alex Facklis helped out with the updates to the *Toolbook* as well. My daughter, Ava, inspired me on YouTube. Last but not least, my black Lab Buddy, kept my physically active and pondering the mysteries of Google on many jaunts through the San Francisco Bay Area.

And a huge thank you to my students – online, in San Francisco, and at Stanford Continuing Studies. You challenge me, you inspire me, and you motivate me!

ATTITUDE

Most books on SEO start with the technical details. What's a TITLE tag? How do you understand your Google PageRank? Which factors in the Google algorithm have changed recently? We'll get to all that, but I want to start this book with a pep talk about **attitude**.

Attitude, they say, is everything.

And nowhere is that more true than in SEO. This is an industry full of information overload, pretty rude intimidators of a technical geeky type, and an 800 lb Gorilla (Google), that would really rather you just spend money on AdWords advertising than understand how you can get to the top of Google without paying it a penny.

To succeed, you'll need a positive, "can do" attitude.

Let's get started!

TO DO LIST:

- Learn from Francie Baltazar-Schwartz that "Attitude is Everything."
- Identify "Can Do" vs. "Can't Do" People.
- Learn to Measure.
- Deliverable: Inventory Your Team & Get Ready.

FRANCIE BALTAZAR-SCHWARTZ AND ATTITUDE IS EVERYTHING

The Internet is a wonderful place, and Google sits pretty much at the center of it. Got a question? "Just *Google* it!" We certainly know the reality of "Just *Google* it" in terms of customers look for companies, products and services. But it also goes for more important questions like the *meaning of life* (*42*), and *what is a LOL cat*, anyway?

For example, Google "Who said 'Attitude is Everything?'" and you'll find out that this quote is attributed to one Francie Baltazar-Schwartz. You can read it at http://jmlinks.com/5i. The point of "attitude is everything" is that you have two choices every day: either to have a **positive**, **can-do** attitude or to have a **negative**, **can't do** attitude.

This relates very dramatically to success at SEO, just as it does to success in pretty much everything else in life from physical fitness to your job to your marriage.

How does it apply to SEO? Well, let's look at the facts and let's look at the ecosystem of people and companies in the SEO industry.

> **Fact No. 1.** SEO is technical, and at least on the surface, seems pretty complicated and hard. So, if you start out with the attitude that you "can't do it," you're already on the path to defeat. If, in contrast, you start with the attitude that you can do it, that other people are clearly doing it (people no smarter than you), you're on the path to success. **Attitude is everything.**

> **Fact No. 2.** Google does not want anyone to believe that SEO is easy. Google is a multibillion dollar corporation and makes nearly 97% of its revenues off of paid advertising via AdWords. **Google wants you to believe that SEO is hard so that you spend money on AdWords.** And Google has a big, powerful marketing machine to propagate this message. If you are intimidated by Google, you're already on the path to defeat. If, in contrast, you have some healthy skepticism about Google (and big corporations in general), remembering that they are just people too, you're on the path to success. **Attitude is everything.**

> **Fact No. 3.** The SEO industry is full of so-called experts, gurus, tools providers and others who pretty much make their money by intimidating normal folk into believing that SEO is incredibly complicated and only nerds with Ph.D.'s in computer science can do it. They want you to stay in a state of dependency and keep paying them the big bucks... So if you allow technical nerds to intimidate you, you're already on the path to defeat. If, in contrast, you realize that they aren't really any smarter than you and that SEO isn't just about technology, it's about words and concepts and marketing messages, you're on the path to success. **Attitude is everything.**

Oh, and as SEO becomes more and more social, you'll want to have an open mind about social media as well. You can really get yourself motivated by watching a 3rd grader (!) called "Kid President" who has YouTube videos with over 36 million views and was actually invited to the White House.

> **VIDEO.** Watch a "Can Do" attitude video by "Kid President" at http://jmlinks.com/5j.

For your first **TODO**, therefore, concentrate your mind and create a **positive attitude**: this is going to be fun, this is going to be educational, this is going to be a journey! Your **attitude is everything** as to whether you'll succeed or fail at SEO!

If a third grader can get 36 million views and meet the President, don't you think you can at least get to page one of Google?

▶ Identify "Can do" vs. "Can't Do" People

In most situations, you'll need to depend on other people. Now the attitude of the people in your team (your webmaster, your content writers, your product marketing managers, your executives…) is also incredibly important. Are they "can do" or "can't do" sort of folks?

Henry Ford, the great industrialist, once made this clear observation:

> "Whether you think you can, or you think you can't--you're right."
> — Henry Ford

In terms of SEO, there are those people who think that a) they can't learn it, or b) it can't be done. And, guess what: they're **right**. And there are those who think that a) they can learn it, and b) it can be done. And, guess what: they're **right**, too.

Which camp are you in? Your team members? Can, or can't?

So for your second **TODO**, look around your organization and make a list of those people who need to be involved with your SEO project. For example:

> **Management and Marketers.** These people are involved in the sense of understanding who your customers are, what you sell, and what the sales objectives are for your website. Your website, after all, isn't an end in itself but a means to an end: more sales.
>
> **Content Writers**. Who writes (or will write) content for the website? These people need at least a basic understanding of your keywords and, even better, an understanding of how "on page" SEO works so that they know where to strategically place keywords on web content.
>
> **Web Designers.** News flash: your website isn't just for humans! It's also for Google. You'll have to educate your web design team that your website needs to "talk" to Google just as much as it "talks" to humans. As we will learn, what Google likes (text) isn't generally what people like (pictures).

Web Programmers. The folks who program the backend, like your URL structure, your XML sitemaps and all that technical stuff. Who are these people and how will you get them on board for the SEO project?

Social Media and Outreach Experts. Social media is the new wave in SEO, so you'll need those folks who are (or will be) active on Twitter, Google+, YouTube, Facebook and the like to be "SEO aware," in the sense of how social media impacts SEO performance. You'll also need people to "reach out" to get inbound links to your website (more later).

Indeed, if you have some really obstructionist "Can't Do" people, you'll need to strategize either how to a) **persuade** them to participate, b) **get them out of the way**, or c) **work around** them.

» LEARN TO MEASURE

As you assemble your team, you'll want to get their buy in on learning SEO. It isn't a rocket science, but it's also not something you'll learn in a day. First, they'll need to learn the basics (See Chapter 1.3). Second, they'll need to learn many of the more esoteric topics as needed. Content writers, for example, will need to be keenly aware of keywords and how to write semantically friendly SEO text. Web programmers will need to understand XML sitemaps and so on. Third, they'll need to be committed to lifelong learning, as SEO changes over time. A good strategy is to schedule monthly meetings or corporate email exchanges about your SEO progress.

Let's also talk a little about **measurement** and **metrics**. One of the biggest stumbling blocks to successful SEO is the idea that it can't be measured. It can. How so?

Know your keywords. Once you know your keywords, as you'll learn in Chapter 2.1, then you can start to measure your **rank** on target Google searches.

Inbound search traffic. Once you set up Google Analytics properly as you'll learn in Chapter 6.1, you can measure your inbound "organic" traffic from Google, including data on inbound keywords. You'll learn how people get to your website, and what they do once they get there.

Goals. Every good website should have defined goals, usually registrations and/or sales. Once you define goals in Google Analytics, you can track what traffic converts to a sale, and what doesn't. (Then you can brainstorm ways to improve it).

When you first start, you'll often have little idea of your target keywords, little idea of your rank on Google, and little idea of your traffic patterns from landings to conversions. But that doesn't mean SEO isn't a measurable activity! It just means you are not yet measuring.

Why is this important? As you set up your team, and establish the right attitude, you want to establish the idea that SEO is measurable. If someone has crazy ideas (like Google doesn't pay attention to URL structure, or keywords don't matter), you can measure these ideas vs. correct ideas (keywords in TITLE tags matter a great deal, keyword-heavy URL's help a lot). Establishing a culture of measurability will help you get everyone on your team, even the most recalcitrant "Can't Do" people to realize that SEO works, and SEO can get your website to actually generate sales or sales leads.

Measurability is a critical part of Step No. 1: **Setting (Measurable) Goals**.

» DELIVERABLE: INVENTORY YOUR TEAM AND GET READY

Now we've come to the end of Step 1.1, your first **DELIVERABLE** has arrived. Open up a Word document and create a list of all the people who are involved with your website, from the marketing folk who identify the goals (sales or registrations?), to the content writers (those who create product descriptions, blog posts, or press releases), to the Web design people (graphic designers), to the Web programmers, and to your outreach team for social media and links. Make an inventory of who needs to be involved in what aspects of SEO, and if possible, set up weekly or monthly meetings about your SEO strategy.

At a "top secret" level, you might also want to indicate who has a "Can Do" and who has a "Can't Do" attitude. You'll want to work to bring everyone over into the "Can Do" column!

Consider having an "attitude is everything" meeting about SEO, and get everyone to stand up on the tabletops and shout: "We can do this!"

1.2

GOALS

SEO, like physical fitness, can't be accomplished without **goals**. Are you training for a marathon, or a sprint? Want to look better at the beach, or just be healthier? Want to dominate Google for "industrial fan" or for "organic baby food?" SEO can tell you *how* to get to the top of Google, but it can't tell you *what* your company's *goals* are vis-à-vis potential customers. To succeed at SEO, you need to have a clear vision of your *sales ladder* starting at the customer *need* and then proceeding to: keyword search *query* → *landing* on your website → sales *inquiry* → *back* and *forth* → actual *sale*.

Let's get started!

TO DO LIST:

>> Define Your Business Value Proposition

>> Identify Your Target Customers by Segment

>> Establish Marketing Goals

>> Deliverable: a Goals Worksheet

>> **DEFINE YOUR BUSINESS VALUE PROPOSITION**

What does your business sell? Who wants it, and why? In this chapter, you'll sit down and fill out the "business value proposition worksheet." A BVP, or "business value proposition" is a statement that succinctly defines what your business does and the value that it provides to customers. For example, a cupcake bakery bakes yummy cupcakes that people want to eat; a dry cleaners cleans people's dirty clothes; and an automobile insurer provides insurance for people's cars.

Here are some more examples, with links to sample websites.

For a New York watch repair shop such as **Ron Gordon Watch Repair** (https://www.rongordonwatches.com/) , the business value proposition is that it provides watch repair services to people living or working in Manhattan who need to get their luxury watches (e.g., Tag Heuer, Breitling, Hamilton) repaired quickly and easily.

For an industrial fan company like **Industrial Fans Direct** (http://www.industrialfansdirect.com/), the business value proposition is to provide quality industrial fans for harsh environments such as factories or farms.

For a San Francisco mortgage broker, such as **Natasha Lovas**, the business value proposition is to help people get cheap mortgages easily. An example website is http://www.san-francisco-mortgage-broker.com/.

For any business, a *business value proposition* is your "elevator pitch" to a potential customer - what do you offer, that they want?

> For your first **TODO**, write a sentence or short paragraph that succinctly defines what your business does and how it provides value for customers. For the **worksheet**, go to https://www.jm-seo.org/workbooks (click on "SEO Fitness," enter the code 'fitness2016' to register if you have not already done so), and click on the link to the "business value proposition worksheet."

» IDENTIFY YOUR TARGET CUSTOMERS BY SEGMENT

Your *business value proposition* explicitly describes the relationship between what you provide and what they want. Now dig deeper: *segment* your customers into definable groups. For instance, **Ron Gordon Watch Repair** might segment its customers into the following:

- Manhattan office workers seeking quick and convenient repairs on their lunch hours (*Budget and time conscious*).
- Manhattan residents who own stylish, luxury watch brands like Tag Heuer, Breitling, or Hamilton looking for expert repairs. (*Luxury watch lovers*).
- USA residents who own vintage Zodiac watches who need expert repairs from a watch shop that they trust. (*Vintage watch lovers, nationwide*).

Similarly, a Las Vegas real estate broker might segment his customers by space need – office, warehouse, retail. Moreover, there might be a segmentation based on those looking to rent vs. buy. And a Miami divorce attorney might segment into men vs. women, those with substantial property vs. those without, those who have children vs. those who do not. A "segment" is just a group of like-minded customers.

> For your second **TODO**, open up the "business value proposition worksheet" and list **customer segments** – customers who differ by type (income level, geographic location), by need (high end, low end, rent vs. buy), or even geographic location. Try to see your customers as specific groups with specific needs, rather than one amorphous mega group. Begin to think about how each might search Google differently, using different keywords.

» ESTABLISH MARKETING GOALS

Moving from business value to customer needs or segments, it's time to think about definable **goals** or **actions** for your website. For most businesses, a good goal is to get a registration / email address / inquiry for a free consult. Our Las Vegas real estate company, for instance, might want visitors to the website to "send a message" about their property needs, or register for a free consult with a leasing specialist. Similarly, a divorce attorney might want a potential client to reach out for a free phone consult, and our watch shop might just want people to call or email to discuss their watch repair needs, and get directions to the shop.

For most businesses, marketing **goals** on the Web usually boil down to –

- A **registration** – for a free consult, a software download, a free e-book, a newsletter sign up, etc.
- A **sale** – an e-commerce transaction such as the purchase of a candy gift tin on an e-store, or an iPhone skin via PayPal.

A well-constructed website will lead customers to an easy-to-see first step. Here's a screenshot from http://www.reversemortgage.org/, one of the top websites for the Google search "reverse mortgage," with the goal marked by a red arrow:

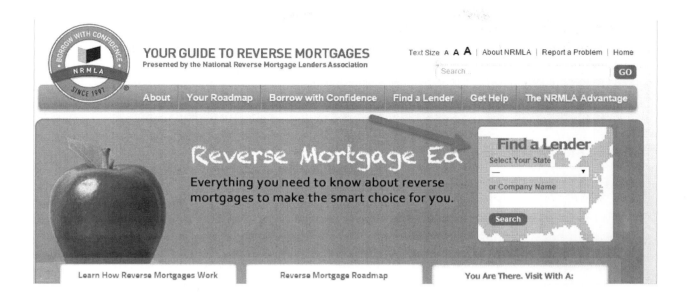

Reversemortgage.org knows what it wants: first, to **rank** at the top of Google search for "reverse mortgage," second, to **get the click**; and third, for a potential customer to start towards the **goal**, i.e. the process of *finding a lender* (and giving the Website his name, email address, and phone number for a sales follow up!).

Abstractly, your process and goals are probably as follows:

1. **Rank high** on a Google search query ("reverse mortgage" in this case).
2. **Get the click** from Google to your website.
3. Once they land, get them to take the "first step" or "**goal**" (in this case, find a lender, thereby giving up their name, email address, and phone so that they can be contacted by the helpful sales staff).
4. **Follow up** with them by email or phone to begin the sales process.

Take a moment and look at your web pages from the perspective of a Google searcher. Does it answer a search question? Is the "first step" or "goal" easy to see? Don't make customers think! Don't make customers hunt for goals, or they'll bounce back to Google and be gone.

Your Sales Ladder

Defining goals is inseparable from defining your **sales ladder**. Web searchers are actively looking for an answer to their query, and they are anything but passive: if they don't see what they want, click, bounce, bye, and they're gone.

*(Some marketers talk of a "sales funnel," a concept I do not like because it implies that customers are **passive**, like little marbles that fall into your website and into your registration or sale. I do not think people on the Web (or in life) are passive at all. I think people as **active** searchers, searching Google, clicking to websites, finding what they want (or not), and being quite skeptical about whether they should take the next action.)*

Let me explain why thinking of customers as jumping "up" a "sales ladder" is a better way to think than "down" a "sales funnel."

I think of *customers* like *salmon* jumping up from sea level in frigid Alaskan rivers, jumping higher and higher up fish ladders (put there by the Alaskan Department of Fish and Game) to get to their goal: the spawning ground. The fish are motivated (there's breeding to be done), and active participants in the process. You can't "bait" them with junk either: they need something good at the end of the process.

A good Alaskan fishery expert doesn't engineer one **huge**, **high** jump for the salmon but rather a series of **smaller**, **easier-to-jump** hurdles that can move the fish from goal one to goal two, etc. Why? Because if the first jump is too high, and too scary, the fish won't make it. Similarly, make your own "first step" non-threatening, and easy!

Make your website goals easy and non-threatening! One of the best early steps in the goal is something **free**.

GIVE AWAY SOMETHING FREE IN EXCHANGE FOR CONTACT INFORMATION

Having something **free** (a free webinar, a free consultation, a free e-book) is a tried and true way to make the first step of your ladder easy and non-threatening. People love free, and will give away their email and phone contact information for something useful that is also free. If you are selling something, think of a free sample or money back offer; anything that reduces the risk of making that first buying decision. Using free, make the first step of your sales ladder exciting, enticing, and free!

For your fourth **TODO**, open up your "business value proposition worksheet" and brainstorm your desired goals (registrations and/or sales) as well as your sales ladder, including the possible use of something "free" to make that first step easy for customers.

For extra credit, begin to think about how you will **measure** these goals. As we will learn in Chapter 6.1, you can use Google Analytics to measure goals such as registrations or sales. But you can also use tactics like special toll-free 800 numbers, vanity phone extensions, and offer codes to track whether someone is coming from a Web search to a phone call into your call center.

Goals and measurability go hand-in-hand.

» DELIVERABLE: A COMPLETED BUSINESS VALUE PROPOSITION WORKSHEET

Now that we've come to the end of Step 1.2, you should have your **DELIVERABLE** ready: a completed **business value proposition worksheet**. This worksheet should define your business value proposition, customer segments, search paths, desired action and sales ladder, and even how you plan to measure customer progress along the search ladder. In Chapter 2.1, we will turn to defining your keywords (which builds upon this knowledge), but first let's turn to the "big picture" of how SEO works.

1.3

BASICS

I like to think of SEO like a **game**, a competitive game like running a marathon, playing poker, or even **getting a job**. Every game has its rules, of course, and if you don't know the rules of the game, you surely can't win. Now SEO is a subject that has suffered from great confusion, with a blizzard of information and even **dis**information from Google and the SEO industry. But despite this information overload, SEO really isn't that hard to understand.

SEO, to use an analogy, is a lot like the process of getting a job. It has its **resume** (your **website**), its **references** (your inbound **links** and **social mentions**), and its job **interview** (your website **landing pages**).

Let's get started!

TO DO LIST:

> Understand that SEO Parallels Getting a Job

> Understand "On Page" SEO

> Understand "Off Page" SEO

> Set Landing Page Goals

> **UNDERSTAND THAT SEO PARALLELS GETTING A JOB**

Let's consider the search for a job. How does the job search market work? People want to "be found" as the "ideal" candidate for a position. So what do they do? Three important things:

Resume - Create a resume. Job seekers create a keyword-heavy **resume** that explains the job that they want to get, and their qualifications for that job. If, for example, they want a job as a BMW auto mechanic, they create a resume that emphasizes keywords like "auto mechanic," "auto repair," and even "BMW repair" by prominently displaying them in the right places, including the subject line of emails they send out to prospective employers. And employers "scan" resumes looking for those resumes that "match" their keywords.

References - Cultivate References. Beyond a great resume, the other aspect of job search is cultivating great **references**. Knowing the boss's wife, having the head of the BMW auto mechanic school, or someone else important or influential put in a good word can elevate your resume to the top of the heap. In short, strong references get your resume looked at, substantiate that your resume is factually accurate, and possibly get you the job interview.

Job Interview - Work on Interview Skills. Once you get their attention, what's next? The job **interview** is the next step towards landing the job, it's the "free glimpse" of what you have to offer that "sells" the employer on making a financial commitment. Notice how a "job interview" is a "free" taste of you as an employee. The use of something free is obvious, *once you notice it* (not to mention the post-Recession use of unpaid internships as yet another way to "try out" employees before really hiring them).

The **marketing equation** is: **resume** > **references** > **job interview** > **job**.

Hopefully you can already see that SEO is a lot like getting a job. How so?

Creating a resume equals creating a strong, keyword heavy website. Your website, in a sense, is your business resume, and it needs to have keywords placed on it in strategic places to "talk to" Google as well as human searchers, and just as with a job search, you have to research the hot button keywords that people are searching for and place those in strategic positions. This is called "**on page**" SEO.

Cultivating references equals getting links and going social. Just as you cultivate references to get your resume elevated to the top of the heap, so you cultivate inbound links, fresh buzz, and social mentions to elevate your website to the top of Google search. Getting other websites to link to you, and social media sites like Google+ or Twitter to mention your website, is called "**off page** SEO."

The job interview equals the website landing. Once you get noticed, your next step is a fantastic job interview. The equivalent of the job interview is the **landing behavior** on your website. Once they land from Google, you want them to "take the next step," usually a registration or a sale just as at a job interview, you want them to "take the next step" such as a second interview or a hire.

The **SEO equation** is **on page SEO** > **off page SEO** > **website landing** > **sales inquiry** or **sale**.

Keep this analogy in the back of your head as you read through the workbook. SEO is a lot like a job search in the following ways:

resume = "on page" SEO = a keyword heavy, easy-to-understand website

references = "off page" SEO = lots of inbound links, and social mentions

job interview = "landing page experience" = easy-to-understand landing pages

Can it be that simple? Yes.

Do most people have bad resumes? Yes.

Do most people have bad websites? Yes.

Does that mean that your resume, or website, has to be bad? No.

Indeed, the fact that most people do SEO badly actually means that it is a huge opportunity for you and your company.

A few simple changes such as placing your keywords into strategic positions on your website can have a huge impact!

You don't have to run faster than the bear, just faster than your buddy!

 **"On Page" SEO**

Let's drill down into the first element, "on page" SEO, the equivalent of a great resume. What are the steps? First and foremost, **identify your keywords** just as you would identify relevant keywords for your resume for the job you wish to get. Notice how in the job search, I have to choose "keywords" that match jobs for which there is demand. My favorite job, for example, is to be a novelist critic working in Mexico on the beach drinking margaritas. However, the demand for *Mexican beach novelist critics* is sparse and does not pay well, and so I have chosen *SEO expert* helping people dominate Google through books, classes, and consulting because there is good money in this occupation.

> *Similarly, for your website, identify keywords that "match" what you have with what they "want" but with <u>an eye to the market demand</u>.*

Then, once you know your keywords, you need to know where to put them.

In terms of "on page" SEO, the main strategic factors are:

> **Page Tags.** Place your keywords strategically in the right page tags, beginning with the TITLE tag on each page, followed by the header tag family, image alt attribute, and HTML cross-links from one page to another on your site.
>
> **Keyword Density.** Write keyword-heavy copy for your web pages, and pay attention to writing quality. Complying to Google's *Panda* update means placing your keywords into grammatically correct sentences, and making sure that your writing contains similar and associated words vs. your keyword targets.
>
> **Home Page SEO.** Use your home page wisely, by placing keywords in relatively high density on your home page and, again, in natural syntax, as well as creating "one click" links from your home page to your subordinate pages.
>
> **Website structure.** Organize your website to be Google friendly, starting with keyword-heavy URLS, cross-linking with keyword text, and using sitemaps and other Google-friendly tactics.

"On page" SEO is all about knowing your keywords and building keyword-heavy content that communicates your priorities to Google just as a good resume communicates your job search priorities to prospective employers. We'll investigate "on page" SEO more deeply in Chapters Two, Three, and Four.

▶ "Off Page" SEO

Let's drill down into the second element, "off page" SEO, the equivalent of great references. Here, you do not fully control the elements (unlike in "on page" SEO), so the game is played out in how well you can convince others to talk favorably about you and your website. Paralleling job references, the main strategic factors of "off page" SEO are as follows:

> **Link Building**. As we shall see, links are the votes of the Web. Getting as many qualified websites to link back to your website, especially high PageRank (high authority) websites using keyword-heavy syntax, is what link building is all about. It's that simple, and that complicated.
>
> **Freshness**. Like a prospective employer, Google rewards sites that show fresh activity. "What have you done lately?" is a common job interview question, and in SEO you need to communicate to Google that you are active via frequent content updates such as blog posts and press releases.
>
> **Social Mentions**. Social media is the new buzz of the Internet, and Google looks for mentions of your website on social sites like Google+, Twitter, and Facebook as well as how active your own profiles are.

"Off page" SEO is all about building external links to your site just as getting good references is all about cultivating positive buzz about you as a potential employee. We'll investigate "off page" SEO more deeply in Chapters Four and Five. Oh, and due to the recent Google algorithm change called *Penguin*, we'll emphasize that you want to cultivate *natural* inbound links as opposed to *artificial* links that scream "manipulation" at Google! It's good *believable* references that help you in a job search, and, post-*Penguin*, it's good *believable* links that help you with SEO.

▶ Landing Page Goals

Let's drill down into the third element, "Landing Page Goals," the equivalent of great job interview skills. The point of a great website isn't just to get traffic from Google, after all. It's to move that potential customer up your sales ladder – from website landing to a registration for something free (a "sales lead") or perhaps even a sale.

So in evaluating your website, you want to evaluate each and every page and each and every page element for one variable: do they move customers up the **sales ladder**? Is the **desired action** (*registration* or *sale*) clearly visible on each page, and if so, is it enticing to the customer usually with something free like a free download, free consult, free webinar and the like?

Just as after a job interview, your family and friends ask whether you "got the job," after a Web landing you are asking yourself whether it "got the action" such as a registration or a sale. Web traffic just like sending out resumes is not an end in itself, but a means to an end!

That, my friend, is the SEO success equation:

> **Pre-search**: identify your customer keywords.
>
> **On Page SEO**: weave these keywords strategically into your website content.
>
> **Off Page SEO**: get links, freshness, and social mentions.
>
> **Post-landing**: brainstorm effective landing pages that convert landings into actual sales or sales leads.

We shall now explore each of these topics in-depth.

2.1

KEYWORDS

If Step #1 is "Set the Right Expectations," Step #2 is to define your **keywords**. Your customers start their quest to "find you" by typing in **keywords** or **key phrases** into Google, Yahoo, or Bing. (For simplicity's sake, I'll use the word *keyword* to mean either a *single* or *multi-word* phrase as a search engine query). Identifying **customer-centric keywords** is the foundation of effective SEO. Your best keywords match your **business value proposition** with **high volume keywords** used by your customers.

- In **Step 2.1**, we'll brainstorm our list of keywords, focusing on "getting all the words" on paper.
- In **Step 2.2**, we'll turn to organizing these keywords into a structured keyword worksheet.

The **DELIVERABLE** for Step 2.1 is a completed "keyword brainstorm worksheet." For now, don't worry about organization. Your goal is to get **all** your possible keywords on paper, and then in Step 2.2, we'll organize them into a structured **keyword worksheet**.

Let's get started!

TO DO LIST:

» Brainstorm Your Keywords

» Reverse Engineer Competitors' Keywords

» Use Google Tricks to Identify Possible Keywords

» Use the Google AdWords Keyword Planner

» Deliverable: Keyword Brainstorm Worksheet

» BRAINSTORM YOUR KEYWORDS

Sit down in a quiet place with a good cup of coffee or tea, or if you prefer a martini, i.e. *anything to get your ideas flowing*! Brainstorm the **keywords** by which potential customers might search for you on Google.

When a potential customer sits down at Google, what words do they type in?

Write down each and every potential keyword search query that comes to mind. You can do this alone, or in a group with your coworkers, friends, or customers. Don't censor yourself because there are no wrong answers.

Begin to "think like a customer" sitting at his or her computer screen at Google:

- **Assume you are a completely new, novice customer.** Assume you know next to nothing. What single words or multi-word phrases (keywords) would you type into Google?
- **Segment your customers into different groups.** What keywords might each group use, and how would they differ from other groups?
- **Are there are any specific "helper" words that a potential customer might use?** Common helper words specify geographic locality (e.g., San Francisco, Berkeley, San Jose), for example. Others specify things like "free," "cheap," "trial," or "information."
- **Don't miss your synonyms!** If you are a "lawyer," don't miss "attorney." If you are a "dry cleaner," don't miss "wash and fold" or "laundry service." If you are an "SEO expert," don't miss "SEO consultant." If you are an orthopedic surgeon, don't miss "knee doctor."

For your first **TODO**, open up the "keyword brainstorm worksheet" in either Word or PDF, and begin to fill it out (hopefully with some co-workers, and hopefully with your favorite caffeinated or alcoholic beverage to get your ideas flowing). For the worksheet, go to https://www.jm-seo.org/workbooks (click on "SEO Fitness," and enter the code 'fitness2016' to register if you have not already done so), and click on the link to the "keyword brainstorm worksheet."

For right now, don't worry about the organization of your keywords. Don't police your thoughts. Write down every word that comes to mind - synonyms, competitor names, misspellings, alternative word orders. Let your mind wander. This is the keyword discovery phase, so be broad!

▶▶ Reverse Engineer Competitors

Next, let's do some searches on Google for your target keywords. As you search Google, identify your "Google competitors," that is, companies that are on page one of the Google results and therefore doing well in terms of SEO. You'll want to **reverse engineer** their keywords.

First, click over to their home page or whatever page is showing up on page one of Google for a search that matters to you. Next, view the HTML source. To do this, in Firefox and Chrome, use *right click*, then **V**iew, **P**age Source. In Internet Explorer, use **V**iew, **S**ource on the file menu. Finally, find the following tags in the HTML source code:

```
<Title>
<Meta Name="Description" Content="...">
<Meta Name="Keywords" Content="...">
```

If you have trouble finding them, use CTRL+F (on a PC vs. Command+F on a Mac) on your keyboard, and in the dialog box type *<title, description,* or *keywords*

For each, write down those keywords your competitor has identified that might also be applicable to you. Here's a screenshot of http://www.globalindustrial.com/c/hvac/fans, one of the top Google performers for the search "industrial fans" with the three critical tags highlighted in yellow -

```
<!DOCTYPE html PUBLIC "-//W3C//DTD XHTML 1.0 Transitional//EN" "http://ww
<html xmlns="http://www.w3.org/1999/xhtml" xml:lang="en" lang="en">
  <head>
    <meta http-equiv="Content-Type" content="text/html; charset=iso-8859-
    <meta http-equiv="Content-Language" content="en-us"/>
    <title>Pedestal Fans | Agricultural Fans | Blower Fans | Ceiling Fans

    <meta name="category" content="Fans"/>

    <meta name="keywords" content="Fans - Agricultural, Loading Dock, Ped
Styles & Sizes At Global Industria"/>

    <meta name="description" content="Pedestal Fans - Agricultural Fans,
From Hundreds Of Styles & Sizes At Global Industrial"/>
```

Read each tag out loud. Notice how each tag in the source reveals the "thought process" behind this page, showing the synonyms "fan" for "blower," plus the "types" of fans people might search for - pedestal, agricultural, ceiling, etc. The goal of viewing the source of your competitors' pages is to "steal" their keyword ideas, and write down any relevant keywords onto your "keyword brainstorm" document.

> **VIDEO.** Watch a quick video tutorial on how to use "view source" to reverse engineer competitors at http://jmlinks.com/5k.

For your second **TODO**, open up your "keyword brainstorm worksheet," and jot down the top five competitors who appear at the top of Google for your target keywords, use the tactic above to view their source, and then write down keyword ideas taken from their TITLE, META DESCRIPTION, and META KEYWORDS tags.

» USE GOOGLE TRICKS TO IDENTIFY POSSIBLE KEYWORDS

After you have brainstormed, it's time to use free tools for keyword discovery. You can find a complete list in the companion *SEO Toolbook* (*Keywords Chapter*), but here are my favorite strategies starting with Google's own free tools.

First, simply go to Google and start typing your keyword. Pay attention to the pull down menu that automatically appears. This is called **Google Suggest** or **Autocomplete** and is based on actual user queries. It's a quick and easy way to find "helper" words for any given search phrase. You can also place a space (hit your space bar) after your target keyword, and then go through the alphabet typing "a", "b", etc.

Here's a screenshot of **Google Suggest** using the key phrase "motorcycle insurance"

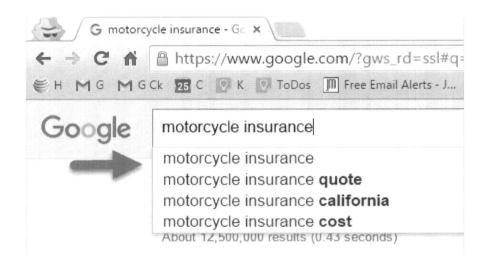

Hit your space key after the last letter of the last keyword (e.g., after *motorcycle insurance*) and more keyword suggestions appear. You can also type the letters of the alphabet – a, b, c, etc. and Google will give you suggestions. Here's a screenshot for the letter "b":

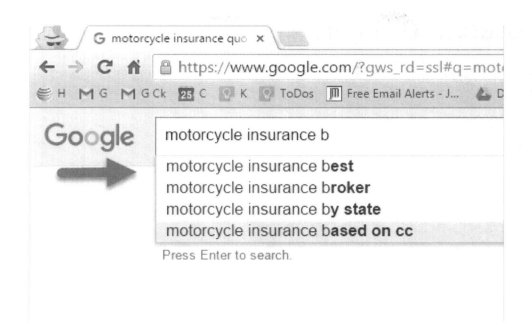

Second, type in one of your target keyword phrases and scroll to the bottom of the Google search page. Google will often give you **related searches** based on what people often search on after their original search. Here's a screen shot for "motorcycle insurance" -

Note the helper words it tells you people use to search: cheap, rates, best, "how much," comparison, cost, and average. Are these not wonderful clues as to how customers search Google?

Ubersuggest

A third party tool that pulls data from Bing search queries is Ubersuggest at http://www.ubersuggest.org/. It basically types through the alphabet for you, and gives you nifty keywords. Spend some quality time with the Google tools as well as

Ubersuggest.org, using your "starter" keywords and looking for synonyms and helper words.

> **VIDEO.** Watch a quick video tutorial on how to use "Google tricks" to generate keyword ideas at http://jmlinks.com/5l.

These three Google tricks are great ways to find helper words, related phrases, and synonyms for your target keywords and key phrases. For your third **TODO**, open up your "keyword brainstorm worksheet" and write down some keyword ideas garnered from these free tools. You want a messy, broad and complete list of the "universe" of possible customer keywords.

» USE THE GOOGLE ADWORDS KEYWORD PLANNER

After you have brainstormed and used the Google tricks explained above, you should have a pretty good (albeit messy) list of possible keywords. Now it's time to use the most comprehensive keyword tool of them all: Google's own official **AdWords Keyword Planner.** It's free, but you'll need a free AdWords account to use it fully.

Sign up for AdWords

To sign up for AdWords, go to http://adwords.google.com/. You'll need a credit card to set up an account; but set your first campaign to "pause," as you do NOT actually have to spend any money. To do this, follow the AdWords set-up instructions to set up your account and then click on the "campaigns" tab, select the checkbox to the left of your first campaign, click "edit" in the menu, and then "pause." (You can even call AdWords at 866-246-6453 and ask them for help on how to **pause your campaigns** – just explain that you are just setting things up, right now, and you do not want anything live). If you're worried about credit card fraud, just go to your local grocery card and get a "gift card" with the VISA logo to set up your AdWords account.

Once you have an operational AdWords account, you can use it as a wonderful way to research SEO keywords.

To get to the AdWords Keyword Planner tool, first sign in to your AdWords account at http://adwords.google.com/. Next, go to the "Tools" tab at the top, and scroll down to "Keyword Planner." Here's how to use it.

First, on the left hand side where it says "Search for keyword and ad group ideas" type one of your keywords and hit the blue box at the bottom entitled, "Get ideas." Here is a screenshot of the button, which is very easy to miss because it is literally at the bottom of the screen:

This gets you into the tool's real interface. This is where you'll do most of your work, and it looks like this:

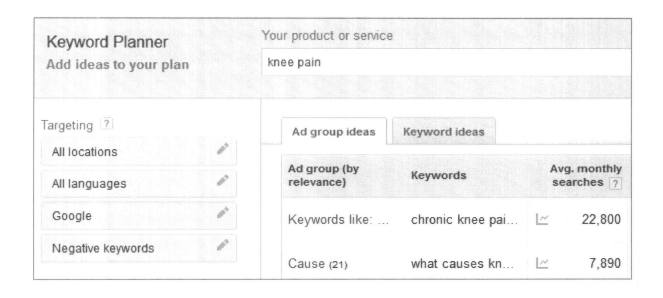

A note to the wise: the Keyword Planner is not going to go down in Google history as the best-designed user interface! To be blunt, Google has done a pretty terrible job with the user interface but because of Google's search dominance it remains the data source for keyword research. Google has the data, and you have to master the Keyword Planner! Just be patient, and click around on the tool to learn its operation and secrets.

For purposes of our example, let's assume we are a New York orthopedic surgeon specializing in knee surgery, and so we'll enter "knee pain." After you click "get ideas," you'll see a tab called "Ad group ideas," and one called "keyword ideas." Scroll down under the "ad group" ideas and click "into" the various suggested groups. Google will give you good ideas for related keywords here. For instance, if you type in "knee surgeons," Google will give you these suggestions:

```
Ad group ideas    Keyword ideas

Ad group (by relevance)

Knee Surgeons (20)
knee surgeons, knee replacement surgeons,...

Best Knee (11)
best knee surgeons, best knee replacement ...

Cost Knee (13)
knee replacement cost, knee replacement s...

Orthopedic Surgeons (33)
orthopedic surgeon, orthopedic surgeons, ort...

Knee Arthroscopy (7)
knee arthroscopy, arthroscopy knee, arthros...

Orthopedic Doctors (30)
orthopedic doctors, orthopedic doctor, what i...

Reconstruction (7)
knee reconstruction, acl reconstruction, kne...
```

Click on any group, and Google will drill down into more related searches. All of these give you great ideas for possible keywords. Note that it also gives you volume information; a rough approximation for how frequently a keyword phrase is actually used.

Next, click on the tab "Keyword ideas," you should see something like:

Keyword (by relevance)	Avg. monthly searches
knee surgeons	320
best knee surgeons	210
knee replacement surgeons	140
top knee surgeons	210
best knee replacement surgeons	390
best knee surgeon	90
knee surgery	18,100
knee replacement	60,500

Again, Google is giving you great ideas of related or helper words (e.g. "best") as well as synonyms (e.g., "knee replacement" for "knee surgery"). Note the ones down that make sense, and write them onto your keyword brainstorm worksheet.

Next, you'll want to play around with the tool and understand some of its more advanced features. Let's start with the columns and pull-outs mean. Starting on the left column, take a look at "Targeting." You'll see here it will default to "All locations" or perhaps "United States." If you click the pencil to the right of "United States," you can drill down to specific states or even cities by typing their names into this space and then clicking "remove" on other entries. This is useful if you'd like to know keyword search volume for specific states; at the city level, the tool isn't very useful as the search volume is often insufficient, however. Alternatively, you can "remove" the United States and target "All locations" which is Google speak for the entire world. Note that to activate a change just click elsewhere on the screen or hit enter. (The brilliant engineers at Google failed to clarify how to enter data into the tool!)

Generally speaking, you'll need a broad geography: so choose "United States" rather than "Tulsa, Oklahoma" to research "industrial fans" or "knee surgeons" as you brainstorm keywords. If a search is too narrow, the tool returns zero data.

The **Negative keywords** feature also has some utility. You can filter "out" keywords that don't matter to you. For example, if we type in "exercises" it then filters out keyword phrases that contain the word "exercises." Many companies want to filter out words like "free" or "cheap," so use negative keywords for any desired refinement.

Columns. On the middle of the page, find the Columns button and click on the downward chevron. Here's a screenshot:

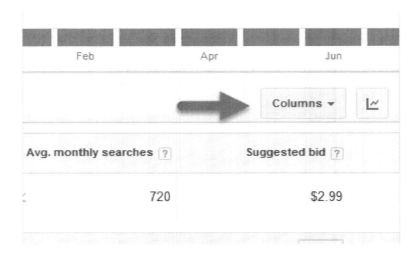

Be sure to click the box next to "suggested bid" as you definitely want this one to show.

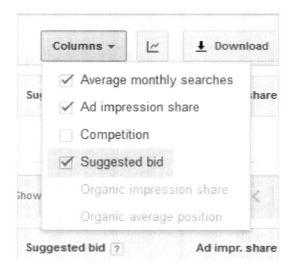

We'll discuss what "suggested bid" means in a moment, but basically it's the average amount competitors are willing to pay Google to get a click from Google to their website via AdWords advertising. I think of it like the "price per pound" of fish at the fish market.

If the "suggested bid" is $2.99 for "knee pain" this means advertisers are willing to pay Google $2.99 for each and every click FROM Google TO their website.

Refocusing the Keyword Planner. You may notice that the tool gives you very broad and often irrelevant keyword suggestions, so I often recommend that you refocus it to just your target phrase and related phrases. To do this, on the left-hand column where it says "Keyword Options," click there, and then select "Only show ideas closely related to my search terms" by moving the blue button to "on" and clicking on the blue "save" button. Here's a screenshot:

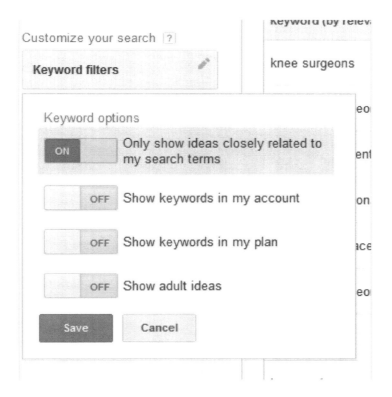

Now click on the column "Avg. monthly searches," and the tool will sort your keywords by volume (the number of searches per month for your target geography). Here's a screenshot of this for "knee pain" after having focused the tool by entering "knee pain" with location set to "all locations," and "Keyword filters" set to "Only show ideas closely related to my search terms":

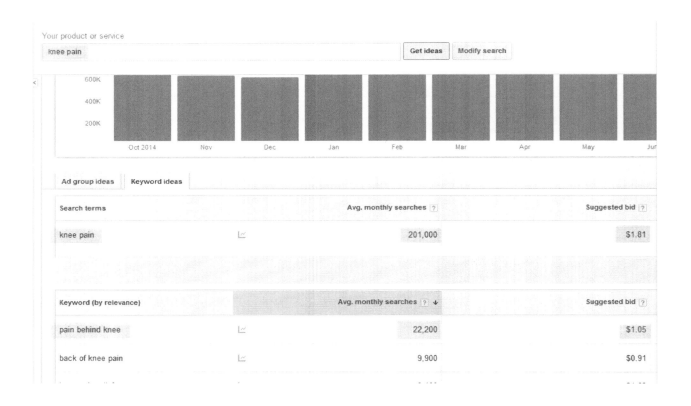

You can see the average monthly search volume for "knee pain" for "all locations" (i.e., the entire world) is 201,000 searches. The number 1 phrase is "pain behind knee" at 22,200 followed by "back of knee pain" at 9,900. **Note that these search volumes refer to exact match only: they take into account only when a searcher enters that phrase and nothing more.** For example, 9,900 people entered "back of knee pain" and no additional words. Similarly, 201,000 people entered the phrase "knee pain" in the last thirty days and no additional words. If they enter "sharp knee pain" that does NOT count in this total.

If you'd like to drill down to a phrase, then you have to re-enter it in the top. Enter "back of knee pain" and Google will give you the related helper words such as "pain behind knee cap," "sharp pain behind knee, etc."

Unfortunately, the Keyword Planner gives only "exact match" data, so you have to manually enter a bunch of related keyword phrases and then tally them up to get a total for phrases.

The Keyword Planner has been strongly criticized by the SEO community for this flaw, because the old Keyword Tool did allow such functionality, but to no avail. So, so far you can only get keyword volumes for exact match. So for now, to compare keyword volumes you are left with manually "guessing" related phrase and entering them into the tool.

You can, however, enter multiple phrases and compare them. Let's set our location to New York, NY, and let's take these keywords:

> knee pain
> knee surgery
> knee surgeon
> knee surgeons New York

To compare phrases, enter them as a comma separated phrase as follows and click "Get ideas":

> knee pain, knee surgery, knee surgeon, knee surgeons New York

Here's a screenshot:

To understand what this all means, let's use an analogy: **fishing** and **fish**. As the SEO technician, you're the **fisherman** of course.

First, you want to "fish where the fish are." This is the column "Avg. monthly searches" showing you that there are 4,400 searches in New York, NY, for "knee pain" vs. only 20 for "knee surgeon" and even fewer for "knee surgeons New York." However, you want to catch yummy fish and the price per pound as set by the market gives you a strong clue as to their value: tilapia at $1.00 a pound isn't as tasty as organic halibut at $22.00 a pound. Similarly, knee pain is worth only $2.60 per click, while knee surgeon is worth $9.07.

Volume vs. Value

There is, in short, a see-saw between **volume** (fish where the fish are) and **value** (catch yummy fish); the AdWords marketplace is telling you that "knee surgeon" is worth MORE than "knee pain" even though "knee surgeon" has far less volume.

Why? Well, think about what each search query tells you about the customer need.

> *A search for "knee pain" might be someone who needs an aspirin (a $1.00 sale at best), while a search for "knee surgeon" is probably someone who is looking for surgery (easily $50,000).*

The Keyword Planner thus gives you both volume and value information on keywords, providing invaluable intelligence as to both "where the fish are" and "which fish are yummy." Your competitors using AdWords, in short, are bidding up the keywords that are likely to end in sales and thus telling you which keywords you should SEO!

Educational vs. Transactional Keywords

Another way to look at this is that keywords that are "early" in the sales ladder occur usually when a person is just learning, just educating himself about an issue and not likely to buy something. These are called **educational keywords** and generally have low cost-per-click in AdWords. Keywords that occur late in the sales ladder are when they are looking to buy something, or make an engagement. These are called **transactional keywords** and generally have high cost-per-click in AdWords. In general, you want to optimize for transactional keywords if possible.

Let me emphasize this:

Identify and optimize for transactional, late stage, high value keywords.

I, Jason McDonald, do not want to be at the top of Google for "SEO." But I do want to be at the top of Google for "SEO Expert San Francisco." Why? Because the former is an early stage, low value educational search, while the latter is a late stage, high value transactional search: someone who wants to hire me as a high-paid consultant.

That said, you still need to rely on your instinct to determine your best keywords and then bolster that with real data from your Google Analytics, which we discuss in the last chapter. The Keyword Planner is only a tool, and the art of SEO still means a lot of head-scratching to identify those keywords that are not just high volume but also high value.

Riches are in the niches

Back to fishing, if you want to "fish where the fish are" (high volume keywords) and "catchy yummy fish" (high value keywords), you also want to find "secret fishing holes." These are keyword phrases that tend to yield good customers yet your competitors have not discovered. They are less expensive in AdWords, and easier to optimize for via SEO (because they are undiscovered). If you discover a "secret fishing hole" vs. one everyone knows about, you have struck gold (to mix metaphors). Don't tell anyone! **Riches**, in sum, are in the **niches** when it comes to keywords and SEO.

> **VIDEO.** Watch a quick video tutorial on how to use the Google AdWords Keyword Planner to generate keyword ideas at http://jmlinks.com/5m.

For your final **TODO**, open up your "keyword brainstorm worksheet," and jot down keyword volumes and the CPC values of relevant keywords. Again, don't worry about being organized. Just get the rough ideas down on paper.

» DELIVERABLE: A COMPLETED KEYWORD BRAINSTORM WORKSHEET

Now we've come to the end of Step 2.1, and you should have the chapter **DELIVERABLE** ready: your completed keyword brainstorm worksheet.

Remember the "Keyword Brainstorm" document will be messy. Its purpose is to get all relevant keywords, helper words, and keyword ideas about volume and value down on paper. In Step 2.2, we will turn to **organizing** our keywords into a structured **keyword worksheet**.

2.2

KEYWORD WORKSHEET

Now that you have a keyword **brainstorm document**, it's time to get organized! Step #2.2 is all about taking the disorganized list of keywords and organizing them into a structured Excel **keyword worksheet** or Google Doc **spreadsheet** that reflects keyword **search patterns** as well as **volume** and **value**. You'll use your keyword worksheet as your "SEO blueprint" for many tasks, such as measuring your rank on Google, structuring your website to tell Google what keywords matter to you, to write better blog posts and so on.

The DELIVERABLES for Step 2.2 are a Microsoft Excel **keyword worksheet**, and a **rank measurement / baseline** of where your website stands for target keywords searches on Google.

Let's get started!

To Do List:

» Create Your Keyword Worksheet

» Deliverable: Your Keyword Worksheet

» Measure Your Google Rank vs. Keywords

» Deliverable: Rank Measurements and a Baseline Score

» CREATE YOUR KEYWORD WORKSHEET

After you complete your **keyword brainstorm** worksheet, you may be amazed at how many possible keywords or key phrases a customer might type into Google! If you look deeper, however, you'll realize that keywords follow certain structural patterns or groups. These *keyword groups* are the foundational building blocks of good SEO. The first step towards building an effective **keyword worksheet** is to begin to organize keywords into groups.

For your first **TODO**, download the **keyword worksheet**. For the worksheet, go to https://www.jm-seo.org/workbook (click on 'SEO Fitness,' and enter the code 'fitness2016' to register if you have not already done so), and click on the link to the "keyword worksheet." Note this is a Microsoft Excel document.

In your own Excel spreadsheet, you'll be filling out columns for the following:

Core Keywords. These are the minimum words necessary to create a relevant search. If you are a watch repair shop servicing high-end watches, for example, your core keywords would be phrases such as "watch repair," "Tag Heuer Repair," "Rolex Repair," etc.

Helper Keywords. Common helpers are geographics like San Francisco, Berkeley, and Oakland. Or terms like "lawyer" or "attorney." In the watch examples, helpers would be "best," "authorized," "NYC" etc. that combine with the core keywords to make the actual search query (e.g., "Best watch repair NYC").

Sample Search Query Phrases. Take your core keywords plus your helpers and build out some "real" search queries that potential customers might use. Group these by keyword family. For example, you'd have a "Family" called "Rolex Repair" and underneath, related keyword phrases such as "Rolex Repair NYC," "Authorized Rolex Repair Midtown," or "Best Rolex Repair Shop New York," etc.

Search Volumes. Indicate the volume of searches (where available) as obtained from the Google AdWords Keyword Planner.

Search Value. Indicate whether a given keyword family is of high, low, or negative value to you and your business. Does it indicate a searcher who is probably a target customer? If your answer is strongly yes, then this is a "high value" search term! Does it clearly indicate a non-customer? If so, this is a "low value" or even a "negative" search term. I often mark simply "hot," "warm," or "cold" next to a family.

Competitors. As you do your searches, write down the URL's of competitors that you see come up in your Google searches. These will be useful as mentors that you can emulate as you build out your SEO strategy.

Negative Keywords. Are there any keywords that indicate someone is definitely not your customer? These negative keywords are not so important for SEO, but if you engage in AdWords, they will become very useful.

Priority Order. Remember the volume vs. value trade-off. "Transactional" keywords (those close to a sale) tend to have higher value, but lower volume; "educational" keywords (those early in the research process) tend to have lower value, but higher volume.

Rank your keyword families on the spreadsheet from TOP to BOTTOM with the highest priority keywords at the top, and the lowest at the bottom. Here's the rub: because of the see-saw between value and volume, there is no hard and fast rule as to what should be your top priority. It can't be just volume, and it can't just be value.

The art of SEO is targeting the keywords most likely to generate high ROI, which is a function of BOTH volume and value.

Competitive Level. Another tricky attribute is competition. As you research your keywords, pay attention to the competitive level. You can guess that a keyword is competitive (many vendors want to "get the click") based on:

- The **suggested bid** in the Keyword Planner: the *higher* the suggested bid, the *more competitive* a keyword.
- The **number of ads** shown for related search queries: the *more* ads you see, the *more competitive* a keyword.
- The *more* you see the **keyword phrase in ad**: the *more* people have "discovered" a high-value keyword phrase, the more likely they are to include it in their ad headlines, and the *more competitive* is the keyword.

Remember, you can use the Keyword Planner to gauge the competitive level. Be sure to click on the Column downward Chevron and enable "suggested bid" and "competition." Here's an example for knee pain, knee surgery, and knee surgeon:

Search terms	Avg. monthly searches	Competition	Suggested bid
knee pain	4,400	Medium	$2.60
knee surgery	480	High	$5.48
knee surgeon	20	High	$9.07

Note that *knee pain* has 4,400 average monthly searches, competitive level is "medium" and suggested bid is $2.60. Contrast that with *knee surgeon*, which has only 20 searches per month, but competition is seen as "high," and bid is at $9.07. *(Remember that this tool only gives you exact match: in those twenty searches are ONLY the exact phrase "knee surgeon." If the searcher typed in "best knee surgeons," that does not count in the total of twenty. Therefore, the tool grossly underestimates volume.)*

If you were a New York City knee surgeon building out his keyword worksheet, you'd want to prioritize "knee surgeon" and "knee surgery" over "knee pain," yet realize that the competitive level is higher for these terms.

Do Not Stress It: SEO is an Art

Don't stress it too much! Your keyword worksheet is a living document. As you build out your website, measure your rank and results, you will "tune" your website to work on those keywords that are high value, high volume, and you can actually outcompete the competition for. It's a process, not a static result. SEO, like cooking or preparing for a marathon, is as much art as science. Don't fall prey to ***analysis paralysis***, and endlessly analyze your keywords as opposed to implementing them.

Search Patterns. Next, let's review structural patterns or keyword groups. It is very important to conceptualize the way that people search, i.e., the mindsets by which they approach your business. Let's take the example of Ron Gordon Watch Repair (https://www.rongordonwatches.com/). This business repairs luxury watches in New York City. What are the basic structural search patterns?

> **Watch Repair**. These are searches built around the most basic search: "watch repair" and in some cases with the added helper geographic words of "NYC,"

"New York, NY" or "Manhattan." These are the more educational, less focused searches.

Micro or Long Tail Searches. These are searches by people who have a specific brand, e.g., Breitling. Their searches are much more focused such as "Breitling Repair NYC." Note that they are "specific" to a watch brand, and "specific" to a geography. And note that by the time they enter "Breitling Repair NYC" they are nearly ready to engage with a watch repair shop.

Branded or Reputational Searches. These are important for your keyword worksheet. Once a potential customer has nearly decided to use you, he or she will often search for you "by name" using your company name and/or helper words like reviews. For example, "Geico Insurance" or "Geico Insurance Reviews." In terms of **reputation management**, you want to pay attention to your branded and reputational searches and optimize for these, so that potential customers see positive information about your brand.

In sum, the **keyword worksheet** for your company should reflect keyword *volume*, *value* (as measured by the "fit" between the keyword search and what Ron Gordon Watches has to offer), and the *structural search patterns* that reflect the "mindset" by which people search.

> **VIDEO.** Watch a quick video tutorial on building a keyword worksheet at http://jmlinks.com/5n.

» DELIVERABLE: A COMPLETED KEYWORD WORKSHEET

After some brainstorming, hard work, and organization, you should have your first **DELIVERABLE** ready: a completed **keyword worksheet** in an Excel spreadsheet. The first "dashboard" tab should be a high level overview to relevant keywords, reflecting the structural search patterns that generate the **keyword groups**, next the keyword volumes as measured by the Google keyword tool, and finally the values measured by the Google cost-per-click data and your own judgment as to which search queries are most likely to lead to a sale or sales lead. Other tabs (which you will fill out over time) include a tab for reporting, a tab to measure your rank on Google vs. keywords, a tab for local search rank, and a tab for landing pages.

Your keyword worksheet is your blueprint for successful SEO, but don't think of it as a static document! Rather, think of your keyword worksheet as an evolving "work in progress." There is as much art as science in SEO, and in many cases, the formal tools like the Keyword Planner only get you so far.

SEO and Cooking

Gut instinct as to how your customers search, especially which searches are likely to be close to a sale, is just as valuable as quantitative research! In fact, rather than think of SEO as a science, I strongly recommend you use other analogies. For example, I like to think of **SEO like cooking**: it has *technical elements* for sure, but it also has *inspiration* and a *je ne sais quoi* of tricks and techniques that you just have to "do" rather than "learn."

In fact, at my Stanford Continuing Studies class, I often have students watch a very fun video on Julia Child and then compare the art of SEO to the art of French cooking.

> **VIDEO.** Watch a quick video tutorial on how SEO is more like cooking than science at http://www.jmlinks.com/5q. Get motivated!

» MEASURE YOUR GOOGLE RANK

Now that you have built out your **keyword worksheet**, your next TODO, is to measure your **rank** on target Google searches. Google rank, of course, refers to whether your website is on the first page Google returns for a search queries. In the industry it's called *SERP rank* for "search engine results page rank." Counting the organic results only, there are positions 1, 2, and 3 (the "Olympic" positions) and then positions four through ten ("page one" positions). Anything beyond position ten is not good. *(Note that because of localization there is also your rank on the local "snack pack" of three local results originating in the Google+ system - more below.)*

You want to measure your website rank vis-à-vis your target keyword phrases, whether you are on page one (< 11) or in the "golden" positions of 1, 2, or 3.

Why Rank Matters

Why do we care about our Google rank? First of all, the Olympic positions (1, 2, and 3) capture the lion's share of clicks; by many estimates, over 60%! Second, being on page one (top ten results) means you are at least "in the game." But third, as good SEO experts, we want to measure our rank before, during and after our SEO efforts to measure our progress and return on investment (ROI). We can also feed this data back into our strategy so that we can then focus our content and link efforts (e.g. blog posts, product pages, press releases, link building) on searches where we are *beyond* page one vs. creating new content for searches for which we are *already* in top positions. In short, measuring Google rank makes us work **smarter**, not **harder**!

You can measure your rank manually by simply entering your target search queries, and counting your position on the first page. Be sure to be "signed out" of your Google account or use "incognito mode," as Google customizes search results. You want to see your true rank on Google searches, not your personalized rank.

Fortunately, there are two great tools for measuring your Google rank, both of which are free. The first tool can be found at http://bit.ly/sitemap-rank . Simply type your domain in, enter your target keyword, and hit search. This tool is a great eye-saver!

Here's a screenshot for "motorcycle insurance" vs. the domain nationwide.com:

The tool highlights the domain and shows it at position #2. Note: if your website is in the *https://* format, the tool does not highlight your domain – you have to manually scan for it.

The second recommended free tool is called "Rank Checker" from http://www.seobook.com/ and can be downloaded from http://bit.ly/seo-book-rank. It is available only for Firefox.

Once the tool is downloaded and installed as a Firefox plugin, enter your keyword list in the tool as follows. In the file menu, select Tool > Rank Checker > Run. Then click "Add Multiple" keywords. Enter your target keywords plus your domain. In the "Options" tab (Tool, Rank Checker, and Options), be sure to check "Don't use Google Personalized Results" and set "Delay between

Rank Checker
The most popular rank checking application on the web.

Queries" to 5 seconds to analyze ten words or less; to 99 seconds if you are going to run a very long list.

(The reason is Google will stop giving you data if you poll it too rapidly).

Here's a screenshot showing how to get to the Rank Checker tool via the Firefox menu:

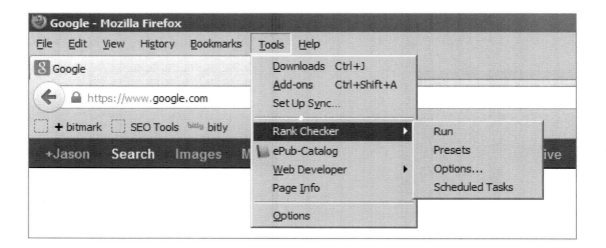

Use the resulting report to identify "strengths" (places where you appear in the top three or top ten) and "weaknesses" (keywords for which you appear beyond page one, or not at all). Having identified your keyword rank weaknesses, you now know where to target your SEO efforts. Blog, build links, issue news - do whatever it takes to elevate your standing for your "weak" keywords!

The free "Rank Checker" tool also gives you more than just a "snapshot" of your Google rank. You can systematically create and save rank reports by keyword, compare yourself to competitors, and export these reports to Excel. In this way, you can chart your absolute rank on Google for your target keywords over time, plus compare / contrast yourself with competitors. All automatically!

I recommend creating a "tab" on your Keyword Worksheet, and listing a statistical sample of your target keywords. Then measure your rank each month, and even calculate an average rank. In this way, you can track your progress month-by-month, and keyword-by-keyword.

VIDEO. Watch a quick video tutorial on measuring keyword rank at http://www.jmlinks.com/50.

If you have money for a **paid rank-checking tools**, I recommend Serps.com, Ahrefs.com, or the Moz tools at moz.com. The reality is that Google does not like people to systematically track their rank on Google searches, so paying one of these vendors a monthly fee for their tool will make your life much, much easier.

Measure Local Search Results Manually

As you check rank, be sensitive to the fact that the free tools generally measure only your organic rank on a non-localized basis. Google "localizes" search results, especially short tail phrases: searchers in different cities, see different results. For example, a search for "probate attorney" in Dallas will return Dallas probate attorneys, whereas the same search in San Francisco will return San Francisco attorneys.

Therefore, if **local search rankings** are important to you, you need to manually check your rank on Google+ local. This is on the keyword worksheet as "keyword – local" tab. There are no good tools to do this; you'll have to manually change your location in Google by clicking on "search tools" at the top of the Google screen, and then "enter location" to enter a location. There are two methods to do this.

Method No. 1: Use Google

Go to https://www.google.com/, and be sure that you are "signed out" of your Google account. (Google also personalizes results, further complicating the measurement of rank). Type in your search keyword. Next, on the far right click on "search tools" and then on the far right, you should see your city. Click there, and you can vary your city by typing in any city you want. If, for example, you are physically located in *Boston, MA,* the default would be *Boston, MA*. However, you can type in *Tulsa, OK*, and change your location to *Tulsa, OK*.

In this way, you can manually count and measure your rank "as if" you were in Tulsa, looking to the three pack listing of Google+ local search results to see whether your company ranks.

Here's a screenshot for "watch repair" with my location set to Tulsa, OK. I have numbered the top three results in the Google local listings.

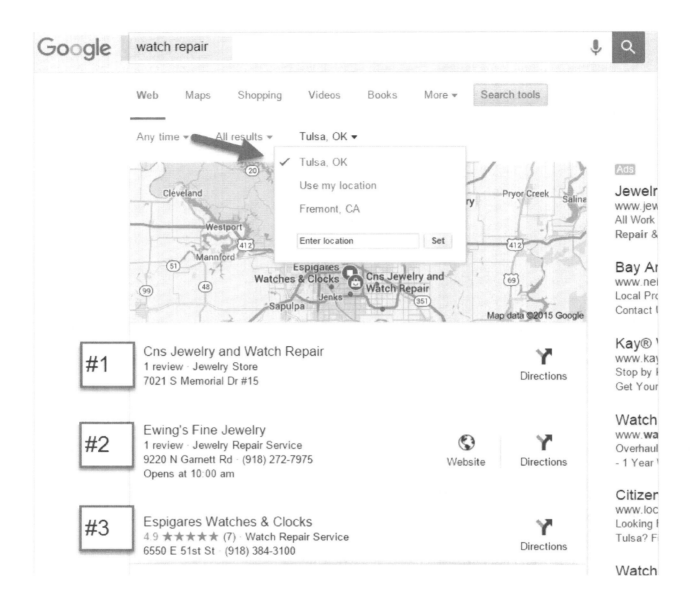

In this way, you can manually enter your "short tail" keywords (e.g., "watch repair," "Rolex repair," "Hamilton Watch Repair") and manually measure your rank in the Google Local listings. (*This is discussed in more detail in the Chapter on Local*).

Method #2. Use the AdWords Preview Tool

The AdWords preview tool is an even more accurate way of measuring your rank location-by-location. Sign in to your AdWords account, and click on Tools > Ad Preview and Diagnosis in the top menu bar. Next, type your keyword phrase into the tool, and then under location, click to change your location to your target city. Here's a screenshot:

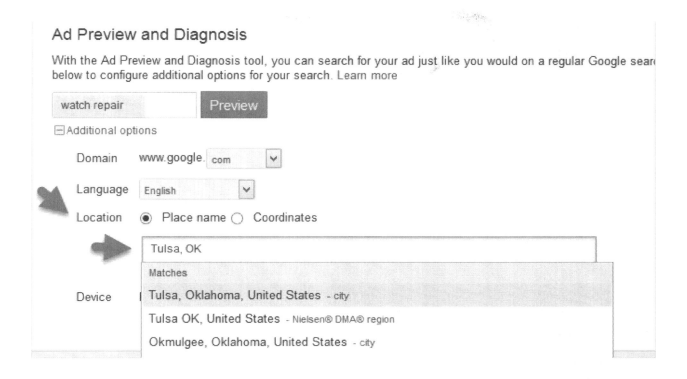

Next, click "Preview" and measure your rank by counting where you are located in the Google+ local listings (usually three). Note that in some occasions, Google still localizes results (showing different results based on location) yet does NOT show the three-listing "snack pack."

Finally, you can also vary the view as desktop, tablet, or mobile phone, and in this way also measure your rank on various devices. Mobile rank does not yet vary as dramatically as rank based on localization.

> **VIDEO.** Watch a quick video tutorial on using Google and/or the AdWords Preview Tool to measure your local rank at http://jmlinks.com/5p.

▶▶ DELIVERABLE: RANK MEASUREMENT ON YOUR KEYWORD WORKSHEET

The **DELIVERABLE** for rank is to copy / paste the rank metrics into the **keyword worksheet** and note the date of rank measurement. I usually create tabs in the spreadsheet and paste ten to fifty sample keyword phrases. It's a best practice to measure your rank at least monthly.

3.1

PAGE TAGS

Once you know your keywords via **Step #2**, where do you put them? "Page Tag" SEO is the quick and easy answer to that question, and it is the most important aspect of **Step #3**. In **Step #3**, you take your keywords from your keyword worksheet, place them in strategic locations on individual web pages via **page tags**, **restructure** your website to send clear signals to Google about your keyword targets, and finally conduct a **website audit** to identify necessary tag and structural changes.

Let's get started!

TO DO LIST:

- Understand Page Tags, HTML, and Talking to Google
- Page Tags and Poker
- Weave Keywords into Page Tags
- A Visual Test for Keyword Density
- Deliverable: a Completed Page Tag Worksheet
- Leverage Keyword Density for SEO
- Set up Your Home Page
- Deliverable: a Completed Home Page Worksheet

» UNDERSTAND PAGE TAGS, HTML, AND TALKING TO GOOGLE

HTML is the language of the Web, and it is based on what are called "tags" in HTML. At a very simple level, if you want a word to appear bold, you might put the "tag"

<strong> around the word such as *"We sell **<strong>**running shoes**</strong>**"* in the HTML text of the web page. This will display in browsers as:

> We sell **running shoes**.

If you are using a WYSIWYG editor like WordPress or Dreamweaver, the editor may do this for you, but behind the scenes the true foundation of the Web is HTML, and the foundation of HTML is **page tags**.

To see the true HTML behind the visible Web, go to any webpage with your browser, right click, "View Source" in Firefox, Internet Explorer, or Chrome. The HTML code you see is the true language of the Web, and this code is what Google or Bing actually uses to index a web page. For example, here is a screenshot of the HTML source code for Geico's page on "Motorcycle Insurance" with the open and close tags highlighted in yellow for the META DESCRIPTION tag and the TITLE tag, which are both very important tags for SEO:

```
<meta name="y_key" content="030608cdc318cedb" />
<meta http-equiv="Content-Type" content="text/html; charset=iso-8859-1" />
<meta name="keywords" content="motorcycle insurance rates, motorcycle insurance quote, cheap motorcycle insurance, motorcycle insurance, scooter, bike, online cycle rate quote" />
<meta name="description" content="Get free motorcycle insurance quotes from GEICO.  Get excellent coverage with a cheap motorcycle insurance policy for your bike or scooter." />
<meta name="google-site-verification" content="Yv_qd4r3MjVMysOkzVkwAfz4S_7Ee2sHQntPTsyHTro" />
<meta name="msvalidate.01" content="5D22D11DDC8CE5612465349DE4140EB7" />




<title>GEICO | Motorcycle Insurance Quote ~ Get online motorcycle insurance quotes</title>

<link rel="stylesheet" href="/public/css/design3/main.css" type="text/css" media="all" />
```

What most people don't realize is that page tags not only structure how a website looks in a browser. **Page tags also send powerful messages to Google about what a web page is about!** In a very simple way, if your page has **<strong>**running shoes</**strong**> on it, you are not just bolding the word *running shoes* in the browser; you are also signaling Google that the keyword phrase *running shoes* is important to you!

PAGE TAGS SIGNAL KEYWORD PRIORITIES TO GOOGLE

If, for example, you write an HTML page like this:

```
<h1>Learn about our Car Insurance</h1>
We sell the best <strong>car insurance</strong> in Houston
```

Which will render in a browser like Chrome, Firefox, or Safari as:

Learn About Car Insurance

We sell the best **car insurance** in Houston

This is doing two things:

1. Telling the **Web browser** to render the first sentence in big, bold letters, and to render the phrase car insurance in bold text.
2. **Signaling** to **Google** that the words: Learn, About, Car, Insurance are important to you – these are words that you would like to rank for on Google.

Remember the "Job Search" analogy? Your website is like your resume. If you are looking for a job as a BMW auto mechanic, then you would BOLD the words auto, mechanic, and BMW on your resume, wouldn't you? That bolding would not only make the words appear blacker on the page, it would also "signal" to the resume-reader that you want to "rank" (i.e., be considered for a job for) those terms.

> *Your Website = a Resume*
>
> *Manipulating Page Tags = Bolding / Making Bigger Keywords on the Resume = signals to Google*

The concept in terms of SEO is to realize that the tag structure of a web page does two things:

1. Talk to "humans" by making some text **BIG**, and some text *italics*, some text a **HEADLINE** and other text just text, some images ON THE PAGE, and some cross-links so humans can click from one page to another.
2. Talk to "Google," by using the same tags to communicate which keywords are IMPORTANT and which keywords are not very important.

Most web designers, in sum, do not realize that they must design for BOTH humans AND Google.

DESIGN YOUR WEBSITE FOR HUMANS AND GOOGLE

Now, fortunately, you do not have to be an HTML expert. Modern WYSIWYG editors like WordPress do the HTML coding for you. Using WordPress, for example, here's a screenshot of my webpage on *AdWords Expert Witness* services:

I have highlighted the Page Title (which becomes the TITLE tag), and the H2 (which becomes the Header 2 Tag) in yellow. The red arrows show where you can change the header tag in WordPress, as well as where the actual header text is located. You can view the actual page on the web at http://jmlinks.com/5r. (Right click, and view source to see the HTML code that underlies the browser-visible web page).

In this way, WordPress makes it easy to "speak HTML" and "talk to Google." You just have to know which tags are important for SEO, and how to get those tags implemented in WordPress. (If you are using another editor, such as Squarespace or Dreamweaver, accordingly, you have to figure out what items in the editor yield what items in HTML).

Finally, if you are using WordPress, I highly recommend the Yoast WordPress Plugin at http://jmlinks.com/5s. It enables you to "split" the WordPress TITLE from the SEO-friendly TITLE tag, as well as easily add a META DESCRIPTION tag to your pages.

▶▶ Page Tags and Poker

By inserting keywords into your HTML Page Tags, you are "talking to Google." You want, however, to do more than talk to Google: you want to win.

But which tags send the strongest signals?

To understand which tags are the most important, let's use a new analogy: **page tags are like the cards in poker**.

Page Tags =

Poker Cards

Now any good poker player knows that the *Ace* is more powerful than the *King*, and the *King* more powerful than the *Deuce*, and that *Full House* beats *two of a kind*. These are the "rules of poker."

Now, could you go to Las Vegas and attempt poker without knowing which cards have which values? Of course you could! The "house" and the other players at the table would love to take all your money. They love it when you sluff away your Aces and keep your deuces!

But you'll do much better if you learn the card values, and some basic strategies.

Similarly, once you realize that Page Tags are like poker cards, you'll quickly realize that you can build a website without understanding which cards communicate what to Google. (And you're website wouldn't perform well in terms of SEO, and it would be like most of the terrible, no good, rotten, horrible, mal-adjusted SEO websites on the Internet).

It gets worse.

Now, could you build a website without understanding HTML Page Tag values for SEO? Of course you could: the "house" (a.k.a. Google) and the other players would love to take all your money. *Google will be happy to take your money by forcing you to pay to advertise via AdWords, and you're competitors are happy to take your money by forcing you off the first page of Google.*

66 | SEO Fitness Workbook

The world, my friend, is cruel.

However, once you realize that HTML tags are like Poker cards… you're next step is to learn their values.

Let's play poker with Google. To begin, examine the following table showing the most important page tags "as if" you were playing a game of poker with Google and your competitors:

Tag	Poker	Comment
<TITLE>	Ace	Most important tag on any page, place your target keyword in the <TITLE> tag of each page. <TITLE> of the home page is the most powerful tag on any website. (59 visible characters; 80 indexed).
<A HREF>	King	Keyword-heavy links cross reference pages to each other, and communicate keywords to Google.
<IMG ALT>	Queen	Have at least one image per page, and put your target keyword into the ALT attribute of the image.
<H1>	Jack	Google loves the header family, so use at least one <H1> per page. Use <H2>, <H3> sparingly.
<META DESCRIPTION >	10	If you include the target keyword in the <META DESCRIPTION> tag, Google will use it 90% of the time. (155 character limit).
<BODY> or keyword density	9	Write keyword-heavy prose on each and every page of the website. Aim for natural syntax and about 5% keyword density.
<STRONG>, <B>, <EM>	3, 4, 5	Use bold and italicize keywords on the page, strategically.
<META KEYWORDS>	Joker	Ignored by Google. Use it as a "note to self" about the keyword targets for a particular page.

Google produces a very good official guide to SEO that emphasizes just how important tag structure is to Google and SEO. I strongly recommend that you download the guide and read it thoroughly at http://bit.ly/google-seo-starter.

Let me emphasize this: download and read the *Google SEO Starter Guide*. It is the best, short, official summary by Google about how to please Google. Here's an insanely crazy idea: in order to get to the top of Google, build your website according to the principles of Google's own SEO guide.

Hate reading? Here are some videos:

> **VIDEO.** Watch a video tutorial of the major page tags for SEO at http://jmlinks.com/5t as well as how to do a page tag analysis at http://jmlinks.com/5u.

The end result of page tags is to understand that page tags communicate your keywords to Google, so your first **TODO** is pretty obvious: weave your keywords into your page tags, starting with the all-important TITLE tag.

▶▶ WEAVE KEYWORDS INTO PAGE TAGS

Now that you know that the TITLE tag is the most important tag, that Google likes the header tag family, that each web page should have at least one image tag with the ALT attribute defined to include a keyword, and should link across to other web pages based on your target keywords, you are ready to write a strong SEO page or re-write an existing page to better communicate keyword priorities to Google.

All Pages Except the Home Page

We will deal with the home page separately, because the home page is incredibly important to SEO and has unique responsibilities. But, for all pages EXCEPT the home page, here's how to write SEO-friendly content:

1. **Define your target keywords**. Using your keyword worksheet as well as the various keyword tools, define the target keywords for that specific page. A best practice is to focus on a single keyword per individual product page or blog post.
2. **Write a keyword-heavy TITLE tag**. The TITLE tag should be less than 80 characters, with the most important keywords on the left. The first 59 characters will generally appear on Google as your headline.
3. **Write a keyword-heavy META DESCRIPTION tag**. The META DESCRIPTION tag has a 90% chance of being the visible description on Google, so write one that includes your keywords but is also pithy and exciting. Its job is to "get the click" from Google. Character limit is 155 characters.
4. **Write a few keyword-heavy header tags**. Start with an H1 tag and throw in a couple of H2 tags around keyword phrases.
5. **Include at least one image with the ALT attribute defined**. Google likes to see at least one image on a page, with the keywords around the ALT attribute.
6. **Cross-link via keyword phrases**. Embed your target keyword phrases in links that link your most important pages across your website to each other around keyword phrases.
7. **Write keyword dense text**. Beyond just page tags, Google looks to see a good keyword density (about 3-5%) and keywords used in natural English syntax following good grammar.

A good way to learn how to write a strong SEO page is to do a "page autopsy."

VIDEO. Watch a quick video tutorial of a page autopsy at http://jmlinks.com/5v.

DON'T OVERDO IT!

Finally, don't *overdo* it!

The Panda Update

Periodically Google "updates" its "algorithm," to improve the search results and combat what is called "Web spam." One of the most important algorithm updates was called **Panda**, and Panda specifically targeted "keyword stuffing," which is the overuse of keywords on a page. In this post-Panda world, the key thing to do is to hit a "sweet spot" of just enough keyword density but not so much as to trigger a penalty. Even more important, don't think of keyword density as a simple numeric percentage, but rather as the strategic weaving of keywords into HTML tags and text. Here are post-Panda principles to writing SEO-friendly content:

1. **Know your keywords**. Keywords remain as important as ever! In addition to your focus keyword, however, look for **related** or **adjacent** keywords. A page targeting "motorcycle insurance" for example should have sentences that also contain words like riding, rate, quote, Harley-Davidson, etc. Use Google Suggest and related searches to find "adjacent" words and weave them into your content.
2. Use **natural syntax** and **good grammar**. Write like people talk, and write using good subject, verb, object. Gone are the days when you could just write keyword, keyword, keyword.
3. **Avoid comma, comma, comma phrases**; another way of saying write normal, natural prose (but still containing your keywords!).
4. **Don't be too perfect**. Don't have an optimized, perfect TITLE and META DESCRIPTION and ALT ATTRIBUTE for an IMAGE, etc. – mix things up a bit.

Post-Panda, the trick is to be keyword heavier than normal English, but still retain good, natural syntax. *A little salt is good in the soup; too much salt ruins it.*

A good litmus test is:

- Does your page contain the target keywords in the key HTML tags yet with some variety and adjacent keywords? And,
- If a "normal" person reads your page, will he or she be unaware that it has been optimized for SEO?

If the answer is YES to both questions, you'll probably survive Panda. If the answer is NO, you are either underoptimized (*keywords do not appear in key tags*) or overoptimized (*text is clunky and weird to "normal" humans*).

Another easy rule-of-thumb. Do your target searches and look at the content of the current "winners." Find the middle ground characterized by the winners in your industry and be as text heavy and dense as they are, but not aggressively more so.

As I always tell my wife on our yearly road trips: speed a little, honey, but don't be the fastest car on the Interstate. If you don't speed, you won't get there first (or near first), but if you drive the red car, right past the cop at 120 mph, you'll get pulled over. Don't underdo it, and don't overdo it (welcome to post-*Panda* SEO content).

» DELIVERABLE: A COMPLETED PAGE TAG WORKSHEET (FOR ONE PAGE)

The first **DELIVERABLE** for Step Three is a completed **page tag worksheet** for one specific page, other than your home page. Take an either a new page or an existing page of your website, and compare it against the desired target keyword. Using the "page tag worksheet," audit the page for how well it communicates the priority keywords to Google. For the worksheet, go to https://www.jm-seo.org/workbooks (click on "SEO Fitness," and enter the code 'fitness2016' to register if you have not already done so), and click on the link to the "page tag worksheet."

A nifty tool to use for this SEO audit is at http://jmlinks.com/5w.

Input your own web page into the tool and check it. The page's target keywords should be clearly and prominently indicated in the tool; if not, you are not correctly signaling keyword priorities to Google! Refer to the *SEO Toolbook*, Page Tags sections for more tag analysis tools.

▶ A Visual Test for SEO-friendly Keyword Density

As you are writing new pages or analyzing existing ones, keep in mind that **keyword density** on the Web is much, much more **redundant** than in normal English writing.

Few SEO experts and even fewer average marketers really realize just how *redundant, repetitious, repeating, reinforcing*, and *reiterating* strong prose is for Google! Furthermore, it's not just about stringing keywords in comma, comma, and comma phrases. The Google algorithm, post-Panda, clearly analyzes text and looks for natural syntax, so be sure to write in complete sentences following the rules of grammar and spelling.

So, write keyword heavy text in natural English syntax sentence, while avoiding comma, comma, and comma phrases. What keyword density is "just right?"

Here's a screenshot of the Geico motorcycle insurance page, using CTRL+F in Firefox to highlight the occurrences of the word "motorcycle":

> Let's Ride® – Get Your Motor Running and Get a Motorcycle Insurance Quote.
>
> Rev up your savings with motorcycle insurance from GEICO. No matter what you own – a sport bike, cruiser, standard, touring bike, or a sweet custom ride, you can turn to us for great rates and great coverage. We even offer scooter insurance. Enjoy the freedom of the open road knowing that the Gecko®'s got your back! Let's Ride®
>
> Get free motorcycle insurance quotes anytime.
>
> Why Choose GEICO for Motorcycle Insurance?
>
> Thought that GEICO was all about car insurance, did you? Think again! We take motorcycles as seriously as you do, and we're pleased to provide you with top-quality coverage for your bike. With GEICO, you get:
>
> › Outstanding customer service (rated 4.7 out of 5 by our motorcycle insurance

How keyword dense is a page? I call this the "pink and pinch test". Find pages for very competitive Google searches (such as "motorcycle insurance" or "reverse mortgage" or "online coupons"), highlight their keywords by using CTRL+F in Firefox, read the text aloud and pinch yourself every time the keyword is used. At the end of the page, you should be in pain! If you are not in pain, the density is too low. If you're in the hospital, it's too high. In terms of metrics, a good rule of thumb is 3-5 % density, but remember also that it's not just numeric density but the occurrence of keywords in normal sentences that matter.

Eye Candy at Top

Text at Bottom

Google likes text, but people like pictures. There is a trade-off between the heavy, redundant text favored by Google and the clean, iPhone like picture websites favored by humans. The usual solution is to put the eye candy for humans towards the top, and the stuff for Google towards the bottom. Revisit many of the pages on Geico.com or Progressive.com and you'll notice how the eye candy for humans is at the top, and the redundant text for Google is at the bottom. A page that does this in a really obvious way is http://www.sfflowershop.com/ (scroll to the bottom, and be horrified).

▶▶ SET UP YOUR HOME PAGE

Page tag SEO applies to your home page, but your home page is so important you should handle it in a very specific way. Your home page is your "front door" to Google and the **most important page** of your website. Google rewards beefy, keyword-heavy home pages that have a lot of text. Think carefully about every word that occurs on this page, and about the way each word is "structured" by embedding it into good HTML page tags. Here are your important "to do's" for your home page:

- ✓ **Identify your customer-centric, top three keywords.** These three "most important" words must go into your home page <TITLE> tag, the most powerful tag on your website!
- ✓ **Repeat the <TITLE> tag content in the <H1> tag on the page.** There should be at least one <H1> but no more than three per page.
- ✓ **Identify your company's major product / service offerings.** Re-write these using customer centric keywords, and have <H2> tags leading to these major landing pages, nested inside of <A HREF> tags. Be sure to include the keywords inside the <H2> and <A HREF> tags!
- ✓ **Have Supporting Images.** Google rewards pages that have images with ALT attributes that are keyword heavy. Don't overdo this, but have at least one and no more than about seven images on your home page that have keywords in their ALT attributes.
- ✓ **Create keyword-focused one click links**. Link down from your home page to defined landing pages around target keyword phrases.
- ✓ **Write lengthy, keyword-rich content for your home page.** You need not just structural elements, but lots of beefy prose on your home page that clarifies to Google what your company is "about."

For good home page ideas, look at Progressive (https://www.progressive.com/), as well as some of SEO-savvy Bay Area medical malpractice attorneys such as http://www.walkuplawoffice.com/ and http://www.maryalexanderlaw.com/. Another good one is http://www.sfflowershop.com/. Scroll to the bottom and notice all the keyword heavy text "buried" for Google to find! View their HTML source and look at how they weave their keywords into strategic tags.

> **VIDEO.** Watch a quick video tutorial on effective SEO home pages at http://jmlinks.com/5x.

» DELIVERABLE: A HOME PAGE PAGE TAG AUDIT

In the next chapter, we'll learn a bit more about how website structure influences Google and SEO, but we can begin the process now by doing a page tag audit for your home page. The most powerful tag on your website is the home page TITLE tag, so start there. Drill down to the text content on your home page and verify that it contains the priority keyword targets identified in your keyword worksheet.

> **WORKSHEETS.** For your **DELIVERABLE**, analyze your home page's existing Page Tag vs. target keyword status, and devise a "quick fix" strategy to improve keyword placement in important tags. For the worksheet, go to https://www.jm-seo.org/workbooks (click on "SEO Fitness," enter the code 'fitness2016' to register if you have not already done so), and click on the link to the "home page worksheet."

Website Structure

Website structure - the "organization" of your website - is a major part of **Step #3**. Whereas in **page tags** you approach SEO from the perspective of individual web pages, in website structure you should turn your attention to how your *entire* website communicates keyword priorities to Google. How you name your files, how you "reach out" to Google, and how you optimize your landing pages all combine to make a *good* SEO strategy, *great*!

Let's get started!

TO DO LIST:

- » Define SEO Landing Pages
- » Deliverable: Landing Page List
- » Write a Keyword Heavy Footer
- » Use Keyword Heavy URLs over Parameter URLs
- » Leverage the Home Page for One Click Links
- » Join Google and Bing Webmaster Tools
- » Deliverable: Website Structure Worksheet

» DEFINE SEO LANDING PAGES

In SEO, a **landing page** is a page you create that targets very **specific keyword phrases**. For most companies, your landing pages will reflect your product or service offerings, adjusted for how "real customers" search for them on Google. Companies in competitive industries like insurance, law, online coupon shopping and other industries where the SEO competition is fierce all use **landing pages** to help get to the top of Google!

Landing pages, however, are not simply about "page tags." Rather, they are always "one click" from the home page, thereby leveraging the home page's SEO power to focus Google's attention on these highly valuable keywords. Behind the scenes, there are also link-building efforts for most successful landing pages.

Progressive Insurance

As an example, let's take a look at https://www.progressive.com/. Notice how the major product offerings are "one click" from the home page, and how the link structure reflects the target keywords. Of special import, scroll to the bottom of the page under "Get Started" and notice the links around target keyword phrases:

> Auto Insurance > links to /auto
>
> Motorcycle Insurance > links to /motorcycle
>
> Boat Insurance > links to /boat

Notice how each landing page mirrors a logical keyword phrase (not just "auto" but "auto insurance," not just "homeowners" but "homeowners insurance"), and is "one click" down from the home page. By "one click," we mean just that: go to the home page, and simply click once on these links: you then land on the defined landing page. Google, in turn, interprets these "one click" links as a major signal of a keyword's importance.

Also notice how Progressive has chosen five, *and only five*, of its most important product lines to feature via keyword-heavy links: *auto insurance, home insurance, motorcycle insurance*, and *commercial insurance*. Each is "one click" from the home page. This compares with other insurance lines (e.g., Segway Insurance, Golf Cart Insurance), which are "two clicks" from the home page via the "more choices" button.

Structurally, therefore, here are your steps:

- **Identify** five or fewer major product lines that "match" your priority keyword phrases for SEO.
- **Build** keyword-heavy, SEO-friendly **landing pages** for each product line.
- Make these "**one click**" from the home page via specific target keyword phrases.

- Relegate secondary product lines to a "**two click**" structure: home page > gateway page> other landing pages.

Check out Progressive's "gateway" page at http://jmlinks.com/5y. Other sites that use this structure are http://www.morenoranches.com, http://www.jm-seo.org/, and http://www.maryalexanderlaw.com/. Notice how each has defined landing pages, and each has "one click" links from the home page to the defined landing pages.

Landing Page SEO

Each landing page should follow the principles of Page Tag SEO: weaving the target keywords strategically into the major tags, such as the TITLE tag, HEADER tags, IMG ALT tags, A HREF tag as well as having strong, well-written, keyword-dense content.

For example, click from the phrase links on the Progressive home page down to a landing page. I like to use the "motorcycle insurance" landing page as an example. So click from Progressive's home page to https://www.progressive.com/motorcycle/.

Notice how it is keenly SEO optimized for the target phrase "motorcycle insurance" plus helper words like "quote." You can see this clearly from its TITLE tag which is:

```
<title>Motorcycle Insurance: Motorcycle Insurance Quotes - Progressive</title>
```

If you "right click," and view the source in HTML, you'll notice the correct use of the META DESCRIPTION, HEADER tags, and A HREF cross-link around keyword phrases. In addition, read the text out loud and you will notice heavy density for "motorcycle insurance" and related phrases. For a model SEO-friendly landing page, you can do no better!

My only critique would be that the page lacks an IMAGE with the IMG ALT reinforcing the keyword target.

For most websites, a good rule of thumb is to identify three to ten priority landing pages, which will each be laser focused on a single target keyword phrase and be "one click" from the home page.

Localized Landing Pages

If your business has a local element, it is often useful to create localized landing pages for individual cities or towns that are "helper words" for your keywords. For example, Stamford Uniform and Linen (http://www.stamfordlinen.com/) wants to dominate Google not only for keyword phrases such as "Stamford Linen Service" (where the business is located) but for those in nearby towns, such as "Hartsdale Linen Service" or "Greenwich CT Linen Service." One method to accomplish this is **localized landing pages**.

Check out the company's home page, scroll to the bottom and notice the "one click" links to landing pages for target cities plus the keyword search "uniform rental service." For example, the Hartsdale page at http://www.stamfordlinen.com/Hartsdale/. Also notice how each landing page is unique, with content at the bottom of each city that is unique and different from the others in the set. Try some Google searches such as "Stamford Linen Service," "Hartsdale Linen Service," or "Greenwich CT Linen Service" to see how effective localized landing pages can be!

Doorway Pages and Localized Landing Pages

Caution: localized landing pages can be considered "doorway" pages by Google, especially post-Panda. You can read the official Google perspective on doorway pages at http://jmlinks.com/6a. The trick for localized landing pages is:

- **Be conservative**: create only a few landing pages for specific cities. Less is more.
- Make sure each has **unique** and valuable **content**.
- **Imagine you are a Googler** reading this page: does it seem to have a reason to exist, other than being optimized for SEO?

To see a company that has gone overboard on this tactic, visit http://www.certstaff.com. For example, go to http://jmlinks.com/6h and scroll to the bottom: you'll see page upon page of city-specific landing pages. This is a dangerous tactic, and sets that company up to be penalized, and completely removed from Google. Be careful! Less is more!

A good tactic is to give "driving directions" from various cities to your home office, therefore giving each city-specific page a reason to exist and making it read as useful for humans. At the same time, you can optimize it for SEO. Localized landing pages are close to violating Google's policy against doorway pages, so please create them at your own risk.

VIDEO. Watch a video tutorial on SEO landing pages at http://jmlinks.com/5z.

Moderation in All Things (Aristotle)

Here is one of the trade-offs of SEO: if you are too *aggressive*, you'll anger Google. But if you are too *passive*, you'll never get to the top. Remember: Google writes the rules to frighten people from doing anything (other than advertising on AdWords).

Speed a little, but don't be the fastest car on the Interstate.

» DELIVERABLE: A LANDING PAGE LIST

Inventory your existing or to-be-created landing pages to reflect your major keyword patterns as described in your **keyword worksheet**. Using the "website structure worksheet" in combination with your **keyword worksheet**, create a list of your high priority landing pages. Each page will then be optimized via page tags and ultimately "one click" from the home page, using a keyword heavy syntax. I recommend a tab on your keyword worksheet that identifies no more than ten SEO-friendly landing pages for your website.

» WRITE A KEYWORD-HEAVY FOOTER

Another tactic I recommend is to write a **keyword-heavy footer**. Take a look at progressive.com, scroll to the bottom, and check out there footer. Notice how the footer has direct links to major pages, all around the phrase "insurance" as in "motorcycle insurance." Or, take a look at my site https://www.jasonmcdonald.org/. Again, scroll to the bottom and see that I have written a keyword-heavy footer.

Your keyword footer should be short, well-written, and contain only your most important keywords. Link FROM the keyword footer TO your target landing pages. The footer increases the site-wide density of your website for your target keywords and allows for "link sculpting" – linking around strategic keywords to your key landing pages.

In addition, as you write blog posts and other content, link FROM the blog post TO the target landing pages, around your target keyword phrase. For an example of this, read my blog post on "Hands on Marketing" at http://jmlinks.com/6g.

Using your Keyword Worksheet and the "landing pages" tab, make sure that as you create new pages for your website as well as blog pages that you link FROM these pages TO your landing pages around keyword-specific phrases. Again, do not overdo this. Just as a general rule, cross-link your pages to each other around important keyword phrases.

» USE KEYWORD HEAVY URLS OVER PARAMETER URLS

URLs or web addresses are what you see in the URL or address bar at the top of the browser. Google pays a lot of attention to URLs; URLs that contain target keywords clearly help pages climb to the top of Google. Here's a screenshot of the Progressive landing page URL for "Motorcycle Insurance":

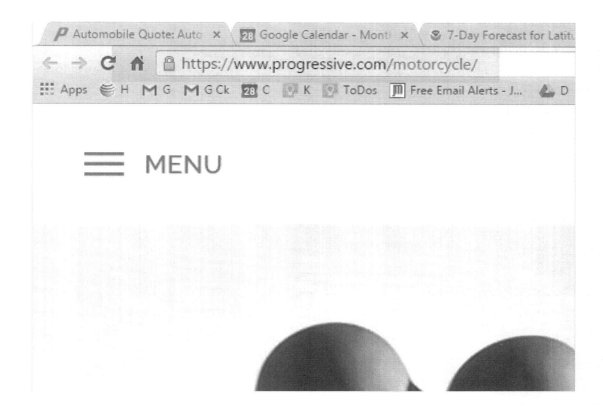

I have highlighted the URL in yellow.

Try a few competitive Google searches such as "Reverse Mortgage Calculator" and notice how the URLs that are on page one often contain the target keywords.

What's the take-away? If possible, choose a **domain** that contains your target keywords. Beyond that, make sure that your URLs (**file names**) contain the target keywords.

Consider these two examples:

> **Example 1 / Geek File Name** - *http://www.yourcompany.com/files/llk1/2/kyoklaol.html*. No "clues" to Google as to what is "contained" inside these directories and files.
>
> **Example 2 / English File Name** - *http://www.sf-attorney.com/medical-malpractice/obstetrics.html*. The domain, directories, and file names all indicate that this is a medical malpractice attorney, specializing in suing OB/GYN doctors.

By the way, what goes for URLs also goes for **images**: name your images after keywords just as you name your URLs after keywords. Rather than naming an image "image215.jpg" have your graphic designer name your images after your keywords such as "medical-malpractice.jpg."

As part of the **DELIVERABLE** for Step #3, conduct an inventory of your website URLs and graphic file names. Are they keyword heavy? Do the visible keywords match the keyword themes from your keyword worksheet?

Parameter URLS

Just as important, **avoid parameter URLs**. Parameter URLs are URLs that contain numeric, crazy, geeky codes such as the question mark (?), percent sign (%), equals sign (=), or SessionIDs (often marked SESSID=), these indicate to Google that these are "temporary" pages not worth indexing. Static, keyword heavy URL's far outperform URLs that tell Google a website is database-driven via geeky parameter URLs.

PARAMETER URLs =
KISS OF (SEO) DEATH

As examples of sites that use parameter URLs, visit http://www.zilog.com or http://dl.acm.org. Both sites have URL's full of session IDs, question markets, etc. Refer back to the Google SEO Starter Guide at http://bit.ly/google-seo-starter and read the section on Parameter URLs. On page 8, Google says:

> URLs like (1) can be confusing and unfriendly. Users would have a hard time reciting the URL from memory or creating a link to it. Also, users may believe that a portion of the URL is unnecessary, especially if the URL shows many unrecognizable parameters. They might leave off a part, breaking the link. Some users might link to your page using the URL of that page as the anchor text. If your URL contains relevant words, this provides users and search engines with more information about the page than an ID or oddly named parameter would (2).

Here's an example URL on Zilog.com:

> *http://zilog.com/index.php?option=com_product&task=product&businessLine =1&id=77&parent_id=77&Itemid=57*

To Google, that URL looks like a mess of information; therefore, this page is going to receive a negative ding in the search algorithm for its target keywords.

Avoid parameter URLs at all costs as Google severely deprecates them in its search results!

If you do have parameter based URLs, **insist** that your webmaster convert them to "pseudo static" URLs. You can Google "pseudo static" URLs for articles on this topic. If you are using WordPress make sure that the "permalink" setting has keyword-heavy URL's.

» LEVERAGE THE HOME PAGE FOR ONE CLICK LINKS

Google interprets your home page as the most powerful page on your website, and as we saw in the Page Tags chapter, you want to have lots of keyword-heavy text on the home page. In addition, you should embed our most important keywords into the home page TITLE tag. Beyond that, you should leverage your home page as a "one click" gateway to your landing pages. It's as if your HTML communicated this message to Google:

```
Home Page > One Click to Landing Pages = Hey Google! These keywords are important to us!
```

Google also looks at the directory structure, namely the presence of keywords in URLs and how "far" those URLs are from the home page or "root" directory. So, in addition to naming your directories and files after your keyword families and high priority keywords, and placing "one click" links from your home page, create a directory structure that is "**shallow**" or "**flat**."

http://www.yourcompany.com/medical-malpractice/sue-doctors.html (2nd level)

is seen by Google as "more important" than

http://www.yourcompany.com/1/files/new/medical-malpractice/sue-doctors.html (5th level)

Thirdly, your home page needs to communicate "freshness" to Google by having at least three *fresh* press releases and/or three new blog posts. Having new, fresh content that is "one click" from the home page signals to Google that your website is alive and updated (vs. a stagnant site that might be out of business), so it's a best practice to rotate press releases and/or blog posts through the home page as "one click" links.

VIDEO. Watch a video tutorial on SEO-friendly home pages at http://jmlinks.com/6b.

›› JOIN GOOGLE (AND BING) WEBMASTER TOOLS

Google rewards websites that make its job easier! Set up sitemaps for Google (and Bing), and participate in their official programs for Webmasters. Sign up for Google Webmaster Tools (now called the "Search Console") for your website (http://jmlinks.com/6c) as well as Bing Webmaster tools (http://jmlinks.com/6d). Then follow the steps below to alert Google to your Google-friendly files as follows.

First, create an **HTML site map** that makes it easy for a search engine spider to go from Page 1 to Page 2 to Page 3 of your website. If you use Javascript / CSS pull downs for navigation, your HTML site map is a critical alternative path for Google to index your website. Second, use the free tool at http://jmlinks.com/6e to create your XML site map. If you are using WordPress, look for a plugin that creates an HTML sitemap as well as an XML sitemap. Third, create a robots.txt file that points to your XML sitemap. (Note: if you are using WordPress, just search popular plugins for XML sitemaps and robots.txt functionality).

Fourth, after you have created these files, submit your **sitemap.xml** file viaWebmaster tools. Pay attention as well to your "crawl errors" and "HTML suggestions." All things being equal, sites that participate in Webmaster tools will beat out sites that do not. Here's a screen shot of how to submit an XML sitemap via Google webmaster tools:

Another feature available in the Google search console is "fetch as Google." If you create a new page on your website, you can login to the Google search console and "submit" your new URL to Google. In this way, you get into the Google index faster and can more quickly climb to the top of Google. Here's a screenshot:

Set a Preferred Domain

You should also set a "preferred" domain (available under the gear icon, top right of the screen). This is because you want to tell Google to use https://www.jm-seo.org/ not http://jm-seo.org. This prioritizes one format for SEO. Here's a screenshot:

Similarly, via your Web hosting company, make sure that the one you do NOT want redirects to the one you do want. For example, if you go to https://jm-seo.org/, it redirects you to https://www.jm-seo.org/. The magic word here is the "htaccess" file, which you can read about at http://jmlinks.com/6f. Generally, I'd ask your resident computer nerd or the tech support at your web hosting company to make sure one, and only one, format is in use.

» DELIVERABLE: A COMPLETED WEBSITE STRUCTURE WORKSHEET

At this point, you have the major components of the chapter **DELIVERABLE**: a **website audit** using the "website structure worksheet," namely:

1. **Your target landing pages**. These are your product or service pages that match common keywords searches your customers do on Google. Inventory the ones that you have as well as the ones that you need to create, and then outline the SEO-friendly content you will write (or rewrite) and weave into the correct tag structure.
2. **Your URL structure**. Avoid parameter (numeric, special character) based URLs in favor of keyword heavy URLs, and build a "shallow" website organization.
3. **Your Google-Friendly Files**. Make sure you've signed up for Google (and Bing) webmaster tools and Google Analytics.
4. **Participation in Google (and Bing) Webmaster Tools**. You should have registered for Webmaster Tools and crossed your t's and dotted your i's in terms of sitemaps (both XML and HTML) and preferred domain.
5. **Freshness Elements**. If you have a blog and publish press releases, great. If not, start them. Make sure that your home page has fresh, new content on at least a monthly basis – the easiest way being to post blog headlines on your home page.

DELIVERABLE. Complete the "website structure worksheet." For the worksheet, go to https://www.jm-seo.org/workbooks (click on "SEO Fitness," and enter the code 'fitness2016' to register if you have not already done so), and click on the link to the "Website Structure Worksheet."

3.3
SEO Audit

SEO, like physical fitness, is all about results. It doesn't matter how much you "know" about physical fitness if you don't "do" anything about it! Similarly, in SEO, it doesn't matter how much you "know" about SEO if you don't "do" SEO! So before we turn to tactics such as content marketing and "off page" SEO, this chapter is a "review." It's a moment to stop, review what you've learned so far, and make sure you've completed the required worksheets.

Remember, to access the worksheets, go to https://www.jm-seo.org/workbooks (click on "SEO Fitness," and enter the code 'fitness2016' to register if you have not already done so), and click on the worksheets discussed so far.

Let's get started!

TO DO LIST:

- » Deliverable: a Keyword Audit
- » Deliverable: a Page Tag Audit
- » Deliverable: a Home Page Audit
- » Deliverable: a Website Structure Audit

» DELIVERABLE: A KEYWORD AUDIT

SEO, as we have learned, begins with keywords. Do you know your keywords? Do you *really* know your keywords? Companies that really know their keywords for SEO understand:

- **Keyword search patterns.** Different customers search in different ways, and keywords self-organize into logical keyword groups. Each keyword group has a core keyword (e.g., "motorcycle insurance") with helper keywords (e.g., "quote," "rate," "cheap") plus some close synonyms (e.g., "motorbike," "moped," "Harley Davidson"). Do you know your **keyword patterns**? Are they reflected in your **keyword worksheet**?
- **Keyword Volume.** Smart SEO experts *fish where the fish are*: they target keywords that have the highest search **volumes**. Have you researched which keywords have the highest volume in your industry, using the Google Keyword Planner?
- **Keyword Value.** It's not just about *volume*; it's also about *value*, especially *value to you* and your business. The Google Keyword Planner gives you useful data on the CPC (cost-per-click) bid on AdWords, but it's up to you to identify "riches in the niches," the very specific searches that are of high **value** to your sales funnel.

Your **keyword audit** DELIVERABLE consists of sitting down with management / your team and fleshing out an organized **keyword worksheet**. Then, measure your rank on Google to set a **baseline** of where your company stands in terms of target Google search queries.

» DELIVERABLE: A PAGE TAG AUDIT

Now that you know your keywords, where do you put them? **Page Tags**, of course. Here are the elements of a Page Tag Audit, proceeding page by page:

- **What is the logical keyword focus of each page?** Leaving aside your very special home page, each page on your website should have a tight, logical keyword focus. Conduct an inventory of all pages on your site, and cross-match each page to a logical, tight keyword query on Google that it can successfully target. Next, audit whether the current tags contain the target keyword.
- **Meta Tag Audit.** The two meta tags that really matter, of course, are the TITLE and META DESCRIPTION tag. Inventory the existing tags vs. suggested improvements to the TITLE and META DESCRIPTION tags.
- **Tag Audit.** Besides the META TAGS, the A HREF, HEADER, and IMG ALT tags are important. Inventory your existing tags vs. the suggested tag improvements.

Having looked at tag structure, turn next to the **content** on the page. As we have learned, Google likes keyword heavy content that is nonetheless written in high quality, natural syntax English. Inventory each page to verify that it has SEO-friendly content that matches the keyword target. Be sure to include related and adjacent search terms to avoid a "Panda penalty" for low quality content.

A quick, efficient technique is to write a short (< 500 characters) keyword heavy paragraph about your company, products, and/or services and paste this paragraph on every page of the site. **Does your company have a "keyword paragraph" on every page in the footer?**

Then turn to missing pages, especially **landing pages**. When comparing your keyword worksheet to your existing website, you may find that some keyword groups lack a matching page on the website. *No bueno!* Add these pages to your spreadsheet, and set a task of creating these new pages to match the target keywords or key phrases.

Note that if your page is template- or database-driven, you may have page "templates" and in that case you may just have to make changes at a template level to improve your tag structure for SEO.

Regardless, the purpose of the **Page Tag audit** is to compare / contrast your pages with SEO best practices to verify that your website has pages that "match" your priority keyword targets.

> **VIDEO.** Watch a quick video tutorial on how to conduct a Page Tag audit at http://jmlinks.com/6j.

▶▶ DELIVERABLE: A HOME PAGE AUDIT

The home page is the most important page of your website for SEO performance, so spend a lot of time working on your home page. A good home page audit works as follows:

> **Target Keywords.** Reviewing your keyword worksheet, what are your most *important*, most *competitive* keywords? Use your powerful home page TITLE tag to convey to Google your website's primary keyword theme, and remember it must be less than eighty characters, with only about 59 visible on Google.

Meta Tags. Review and revise not only your TITLE tag but also your META DESCRIPTION tag, including high priority keywords and making sure that you respect the META DESCRIPTION character limit of 155 characters.

Home Page Content. Google pays a lot of attention to the text on your home page, so verify that the keywords on your keyword worksheet actually appear at least once on your home page. At the same time, do not clutter your home page so much that it doesn't look good "for humans." *The art of SEO is to combine the keyword heavy text that Google likes, with the pretty visuals that humans like.* This is especially true for the home page, so put pictures, graphics, and actions at the top of the page, and keyword heavy text for Google at the bottom.

One Click to Landing Pages. It should be "one click" down from your home page to your priority landing pages, so inventory whether a) your landing pages exist, and b) whether they are "one click" from the home page.

VIDEO. Watch a quick video tutorial on how to conduct a Home Page audit at http://jmlinks.com/6k.

» DELIVERABLE: A WEBSITE STRUCTURE AUDIT

As we learned in the Chapter on Website Structure, there are do's and don'ts for structural SEO:

Do include keywords in your URLs. Are your existing URL's keyword heavy? Do your domains, directories, file names and even graphic names contain keywords?

Don't use parameter URLs. Inventory your existing URLs and look for question marks (?), percentage signs (%), and session IDs. All are very negative for SEO, and if they exist, have your webmaster or programmer transition to static or *pseudostatic* URLs as soon as possible.

Do sculpt your links. A strong SEO website uses internal link syntax to talk to Google. Your home page should have keyword heavy "one click" links down from the home page to your landing pages. Similarly, your site navigation should be keyword heavy and "sculpt" your links around keyword phrases.

Finally, make sure that your website contains your **Google friendly files**, especially a robots.txt file, an XML sitemap, and an HTML sitemap. Every page should link to the HTML sitemap, and the HTML sitemap in turn should have keyword-heavy links to all derivative pages. This important file makes it easy for the Googlebot to crawl your website.

Join **Google Webmaster Tools** to be part of the Google "Mickey Mouse Club" and get insider information on how Google perceives your website!

Now that you've completed these DELIVERABLES, it's time to move to our next step, **Step #4: Create Content**.

4.1

CONTENT SEO

In **Step #1**, you defined your goals; in **Step #2**, you identified your keywords; and in **Step #3**, you structured your pages and website to talk to Google about your target keywords. In **Step #4**, you begin to populate your SEO-friendly website with keyword heavy content.

Content, after all, is king.

But let's be clear. Just throwing content up on your website willy-nilly won't help your SEO! Why? Well, for one, we've already learned that *well structured content* (SEO-friendly page tags, SEO-friendly website structure) is critical for success at SEO.

In **Step #4**, we will expand on this by creating an **SEO Content Marketing Strategy** ("Content SEO" for short) built upon your keyword targets.

Content SEO is all about creating web pages that *match* Google search *queries* with compelling, relevant *content,* be that on a specific web page, a press release, or a blog post. **Content SEO** is all about creating an on-going process (daily, weekly, monthly) of creating compelling SEO-friendly content for your website.

Let's get started!

TO DO LIST:

>> Identify Keyword Themes

>> Create a Content Map

>> Set up a Blog

>> Create a Content Marketing Plan

>> Deliverable: a Content Marketing Plan

» IDENTIFY KEYWORD THEMES

Every successful website has keyword **themes** just as every successful company or organization has a **focus**. You don't produce *everything*, nor do your target searchers search Google for *everything*. You **focus**, and they **focus**. If you are Safe Harbor CPAs (http://www.safeharborcpa.com/), a CPA firm in San Francisco, for example, your target customers search Google for things like "San Francisco CPA Firms," "Business CPAs in San Francisco, CA," or keyword specific searches such as "CPA Firm for IRS Audit Defense in SF," or "FBAR Tax Issues." Guess what? Safe Harbor CPAs has matching content on its website for each of those queries, including an active blog, and that's no accident!

If you are a Houston probate attorney, you'll need lots of content about "Houston" and about "probate" plus related terms like estate planning, guardianships, and wills. Take a look at http://www.fordbergner.com/ and – guess what – that site has well-optimized content, including an up-to-date blog, on exactly those keyword themes.

If **keyword discovery** is about organizing your SEO strategy around keyword themes, then **Content SEO**, in turn, is about creating a strategy to produce the type of content that "matches" your keyword themes.

MATCH CONTENT TO SEARCH QUERIES

The first step is to organize your keyword themes onto your keyword worksheet. Among the most common themes are:

Branded Searches. Searches in which customers already know your company, and simply use Google to find you quickly. In the example of Safe Harbor CPAs, a branded Google search is literally "Safe Harbor CPAs," while for Ford Bergner Law Firm it is "Ford Bergner."

Anchor Searches. Searches in which a core customer need matches a core product. In the example of Safe Harbor CPAs, an anchor search would be "San

Francisco CPA Firms," or "Tax Preparation San Francisco." For a large company like Progressive Insurance, the anchor searches are "Auto Insurance" or "Motorcycle Insurance."

Keyword Specific Searches / Long Tail. Searches that are usually (but not always) long tail searches (multiple search keywords), and reflect a very focused customer need. For example, "IRS Audit Defense CPA in San Francisco" or "motorcycle insurance quotes online" vs. just "CPA Firm."

Keyword Specific Searches / Micro Searches. Short but micro-focused search queries such as "Tag Heuer Repair," or "Breitling Repair," or "AdWords Coupons." These are short but very specific search queries.

News and Trending Searches. These are searches reflecting industry news, trends, and buzz. For example, with recent IRS initiatives to crack down on overseas assets, a search such as "2012 OVDP Program" reflects an awareness of the 2012 "Offshore Voluntary Disclosure Program." "FBAR" is another one, focusing on foreign asset disclosure requirements.

These are not the only types of keyword queries that might exist; just the most common.

Many SEO content experts also distinguish between *evergreen* keywords (keywords that are always valuable such as "CPA San Francisco") vs. *time-sensitive* content (such as "2015 Tax Changes). And don't forget the difference between *educational* search queries and *transactional* search queries ("knee pain" vs. "best knee surgeon in San Francisco"). Finally, there is *link bait* content (such as infographics, or tutorial posts), designed to attract links, and of course *social media content*, especially content that is designed to be highly shareable on networks like Facebook or Twitter.

Regardless of the target keywords, the basic goal is to map out the types of content that are most relevant to you and your customers, and to start a content marketing process that generates highly relevant content on a regular basis.

Once your site is well optimized for SEO, you can often see the basic patterns directly in Google Analytics under *Acquisition > Keywords > Organic*. You can also see them in Webmaster tools at *Search Traffic > Search queries*. Bing's Webmaster tools service also gives you data about the actual search queries that result in real traffic to your website. **Note**: both Google and Bing are increasingly reluctant to share keyword data, and so you must often "extrapolate" the actual search query based on the landing page first touched by a Web surfer.

For your first **TODO**, review your **keyword worksheet**, brainstorm your keyword patterns, check Google Analytics, Google Search Console, and Bing Webmaster Tools for keywords, then group your keyword families into patterns that reflect **branded search**, **anchor search**, **esoteric search**, and **news search**. If there are other relevant patterns, indicate those as well.

▶▶ CREATE A CONTENT MAP

Now that you have your keyword themes, it's time to brainstorm the types of content you are going to create that will match the relevant keyword theme. Your second **TODO** is to create a **content map**. In a sense, you are "reverse engineering" the process of Google search: taking what people search on Google as your **end point**, and creating the type of content that has a good chance of appearing in Google search results as your **starting point**. Your **content map** will map your keyword themes to the relevant locations on your website.

Here's a table mapping out how keyword themes are generally reflected on website locations:

Keyword Theme	Website Location	Comments on Content SEO
Branded Searches	Home Page, About You, Testimonial Pages	Branded search is all about making sure you show up for your own name as well as commonly appended helper words like "reviews." Make sure that at least some TITLE tags communicate your name, and your "about" page is focused on branded search. Don't forget branded search for key company employees (JM Internet Group vs. Jason McDonald, for example).
Anchor Searches	Home Page, Landing Pages, Product Pages (High Level)	Anchor search terms generally reflect your product categories in the format that customers search. Revisit *progressive.com*, for example, and you'll see how each anchor search query is reflected in a focused **landing page**. In addition, the site navigation and links are "sculpted" around keywords to pull Google up to the target landing pages.
Keyword Specific Searches	Product sub pages, blog posts.	Your esoteric searches are generally long tail searches, and/or searches for very niche, focused products or services ("micro" searches). These are less competitive than anchor searches and are well served by content on product sub pages as well as blog posts.
News Searches	Press releases, blog posts	Every industry has news, buzz, and timely

		topics! The place to put this content is generally either in a press release on your website, and/or a blog post.

For your second **TODO**, take your keyword themes and map out where they should be reflected on your website into your **content map**. I recommend doing this in Excel. Check your rank on Google searches vs. relevant search queries for each type – if you are not on page one, or not in the top three positions for a query... you have work to do!

In some cases, you may have *missing* elements (for example, you don't have blog or don't produce press releases); in others you may have the elements there *already* (product specific pages, for example) but their content is not SEO-friendly (has poorly defined TITLE tags, content does not reflect logical keyword target, etc.). Regardless, you are mapping your keyword themes to the logical locations on your website with the goal of getting into a rhythm or content creation process of creating SEO-friendly content on a regular basis.

» SET UP A BLOG

To succeed at SEO, you must have a blog! A blog helps your SEO efforts in these important ways:

- **Micro-specific Content**. Whereas your major landing pages must reflect "anchor" searches, your blog can have a nearly infinite number of pages tied together by keyword themes. Your blog gives you the easy ability to create a lot of content and match that content on the many small, fragmented and long-tail searches that make up today's search behavior. Often you might not win on the "major" searches but you can make up for this by winning on the "micro" searches, many of which will be low volume but high value.
- **Freshness**. Google rewards sites that have new, fresh content. Having a blog gives you an easy way to churn out fresh content and send a freshness signal to Google: we're alive, we're alive, we're alive... I recommend at least four blog posts per month for this reason.
- **Website Size**. Size matters! (*Didn't see that joke coming, did you?*). Given the choice between Pizza restaurant No. 1 with 10 web pages, and Pizza restaurant No. 2 with 1000 pages, Google will prefer the larger website: *it must be more important because it has more content*. A blog allows you to expand the size your web content.

The best blog platform, by far, is **WordPress**. If you do not already have a blog, touch base with your Web developer and insist that he or she set up a blog for you. Major providers such as GoDaddy have easy-to-use, out-of-the-box WordPress packages. As you blog on WordPress, be sure to "tag" each blog post with keyword themes that reflect your keyword targets (as identified on your keyword worksheet).

Take a look at our blog at https://www.jm-seo.org/blog for examples of best blogging practices for SEO, including tagging blog posts based on keyword themes. Here's a screenshot of our WordPress "tag cloud," located at the far left of every page on our blog:

TAGS

AdWords AdWords Books Arizona Austin Book Reviews Books Business California Content Marketing Directory Display Network Free Tools Google Google Algorithm Google Analytics Google Local Houston Keyword Planner Keywords Local SEO Los Angeles Marketing Metrics Mobile-friendly Mobile SEO New York New York City Photography Remarketing Retargeting San Francisco SEO SEO Books SEO Tips SEO Training Small Business Social Media Social Media Marketing Texas Top Tens Tucson Twitter Marketing Viral Marketing WordPress SEO Yelp

Notice how our WordPress tags reflect our target keywords such as AdWords, SEO, and Social Media Marketing as indicated with a bigger font, meaning more blog content. To learn more about WordPress tags, please visit http://jmlinks.com/6n.

Blog Hosting

Note that it is better to host your blog on your own site (http://www.company.com/blog) than on another site (http://company.wordpress.com/). However, the "Perfect is the enemy of the Good" (Voltaire), so if you can't host on your own domain, host on another platform. For a quick blogging platform, I prefer Blogger (http://www.blogger.com) to WordPress.com (http://www.wordpress.com), as the former is very SEO-friendly while the latter (ironically) is not, and has many obnoxious lock-ins to prevent you from porting your blog to your own site at a later time. (Note: just to confuse you, *Wordpress.org* is the site for the free software (good), whereas *WordPress.com* is a revenue-generating site (bad)).

> **VIDEO.** Watch a quick video tutorial on SEO-friendly blogging at http://jmlinks.com/6m.

» DELIVERABLE: A CONTENT MARKETING PLAN

Now that you have a **content map** of your website vs. your keyword themes on your **keyword worksheet**, you are ready to produce your **DELIVERABLE**: a **content marketing plan**. Your content marketing plan will consist of these basic phases.

> **Phase 1: Quick Fix**. Based on your keyword worksheet including the content map, conduct an inventory of existing pages. Adjust their TITLE tags, META DESCRIPTION tags, and content to bring that content into alignment with your logical Google searches. I usually also write a "keyword paragraph" and place on all website pages to increase keyword density and allow for link sculpting. Don't forget to optimize the content of that all-important home page!
>
> **Phase 2: Content Inventory**. Are you missing anything? Often times, there will be a very important keyword pattern that has no corresponding landing page, for example. Or your site will not have a blog, or you will have never set up a press release system. Inventory what you are missing and start to prioritize what needs to be done to get that content on your website. Commonly needed elements are:
>
> - **Blog**. I recommend at least four blog posts per month; these can be on easy, man-on-the-street type themes but you really need to commit to at least four, and make sure that they are relevant vis-a-vis your keyword themes.
> - **Press Releases**. As discussed below, I recommend at least two per month and (if possible), use the CISION / PRWEB system to syndicate them (cost is approximately $350 / month).

- **Anchor Pages**. Make sure that each major search has a corresponding anchor page.
- **Anchor Content**. Consider writing the "ultimate" guide to such-and-such or a provocative, and useful eBook. This is great to a) attract links, and b) to acquire customer email addresses and contact information. Most companies need to commit to one, and only one, type of anchor content.

Phase 3: Content Creation Process. Once you have done the Quick Fix to the website and created any missing landing pages, set up a blog, and/or set up a press releases system, you need to create a content creation schedule and process. This is an assessment of who will do what, when, where, and how to create the type of on-going content that Google and Web searchers will find attractive.

WORKSHEETS. For your **DELIVERABLE**, fill out the "content marketing worksheet," specifically each phase. For the worksheet, go to https://www.jm-seo.org/workbooks (click on "SEO Fitness," and enter the code 'fitness2016' to register if you have not already done so), and click on the link to the "content marketing worksheet."

4.2
Press Releases

After you've created your anchor or landing page content, press releases should be a major part of your **SEO Content** strategy. Why? Because Google rewards sites that have fresh content!

Here are the reasons. First, websites that have new, fresh content (for example, a press release or blog post put up in the last week) are clearly more "alive" than websites that never get updated. We live in a fast-paced world, and users want the *latest* iPhone software, the *latest* news about Obamacare, and the *latest* nutritional supplement. Google wants to give users the latest and greatest on any topic as well. Second, fresh content signals to Google that your website and business are still alive vs. the many "walking dead" websites that reflect businesses dead or dying in this age of recession. And third, press releases have a unique SEO advantage: **syndication**. Free and paid syndication services like PRLog.org or PRWeb.com connect with blogs, portals, other websites and even Twitter feeds to push your press releases across the Web, creating inbound buzz and backlinks which Google interprets as signs of community authority. Press release SEO, in short, gives a three-for-one benefit!

Let's get started!

To Do List:

- » Make a Press Release Calendar
- » Upload Your SEO-Friendly Press Releases
- » Leverage Free Press Release Syndication Services
- » Deliverables: Press Release Worksheet

▶▶ MAKE A PRESS RELEASE CALENDAR

What can make a good press release? **Almost anything**. Keep your keyword worksheet in mind and look for press release opportunities around your company. I recommend you create a **press release calendar** of opportunities.

For your first **TODO**, open up a Word document, title it "Press Release Calendar," and write down a list of possible press release topics and dates of the release. For example:

Sample Press Release Topic:	When To Release:
New product or service	Every time you have a new product or service, generate a press release.
Annual Trade Show	Generate a press release before the annual trade show, as well as after announcing your participation to celebrate your success.
Personnel Changes	Generate a press release for every major corporate hire.
New website content	Generate a press release after any major blog post, list of "top seven resources," infographic, etc.
Partnership Announcements	Generate a press release after any cooperative partnership with a company or supplier.
Industry Awards or Milestones	Any time you win an industry award or cross a milestone (such as the 1000th follower on Twitter), it's time for a press release!

Your **press release calendar** will help keep you focused, and tie your press release opportunities to your keyword worksheet. The goal is to avoid writer's block and get into a rhythm of at least two press releases per month, minimum.

Once you have an idea in hand, here are the steps to create a press release:

1. Identify the **press release idea**. Realize that a press release can be not only a new product or a new technology but something as simple as your participation in a trade show, an event that you may be having, a new hire, new inventory, or even your commentary on an industry trend. **Literally, anything new can become a press release!**

2. Connect the press release idea to a **target keyword** from your keyword worksheet. The point of generating press releases, after all, is to improve keyword performance.
3. Create a **press release** using your SEO page template and follow "**SEO best practices**" for on page SEO (see below).
4. **Upload** the press release to your website, be sure that your website has a press release section with each press release on an independent URL, and include a "one click" link from the home page to the press release.
5. Leverage free and/or paid **syndication services** to proliferate mentions of your press releases around the Internet.

›› Upload Your SEO-Friendly Press Releases

Double-check your press release to make sure that it follows "on page" SEO best practices. Here's your checklist:

Item	SEO Page Tag Structure
Pithy, exciting headline	<TITLE> tag
First paragraph with "main idea"	<META DESCRIPTION> tag and first paragraph. Include a link to your website in the first paragraph usually around a keyword phrase.
Target URL	A target URL on your website, to which you want to attract Google. Embed this in the first paragraph, and have it as a "naked" URL (http://) format in the third paragraph.
Several paragraphs describing your news and an image.	Write keyword heavy copy and include at least one image with ALT attribute.
Contact information for more info.	Embedded URL early in the press release, set up in http:// format plus contact information at the end of the release

In other words, follow your HTML page tag template to optimize your press release in terms of its on-page SEO. Be sure to embed your target keywords in your <TITLE> tag, and use best SEO practices like the H1 family, <B>, <STRONG>, ALT attributes, for images etc. Write **keyword-heavy** text for the press release body! Make sure that it has a snappy <TITLE> and a snappy META DESCRIPTION / first paragraph so that people will be interested in "reading more."

At the website structure level, your best practice is to have a directory called "news" as in *http://www.yourcompany.com/news/* and to host each press release in HTML linked to from a primary news gateway page. I also recommend that you run at least three press releases on your home page, with "one click" links down to each new press release. All of this freshens your website and pulls Google into your new content.

Good examples of press releases can be found at https://www.jm-seo.org/category/press-releases/ as well as http://www.qnx.com/news/.

> **VIDEO.** Watch a quick video tutorial on how to write an SEO-friendly press release at http://jmlinks.com/6p.

Important Changes, Post Penguin

Before the Penguin update to Google, you could use Press Releases to "optimize" your inbound links. For example, you'd create a bunch of press releases all linking back to your site around the phrase "industrial fans" or "motorcycle insurance." This manipulation did not make Google happy, so the search giant pressured the major services to add the NOFOLLOW tag to their releases, which nullified much of this benefit, as part of the so-called Penguin algorithm update.

Thus, for a short while, press releases had little impact on SEO. However, there is always another turn of the screw. Now, despite the fact that press release URL's remain "nofollow" in most circumstances, Google does tend to reward sites that issue them. (Trust me: I know this based on client experiments; the reason probably being that in many industries, Google has so few links to choose from among competing sites that the sheer quantity of press release links can be sufficient to help a site get to the top).

In addition, if you use ONLY the *http://* format for your clickable links, there are still a small percentage of sites that retain the DOFOLLOW link structure. So be sure to include links FROM the press release BACK to your site in the format of http://www.company.com. The reality is that Google is often forced to choose not between two GREAT sites to rank for a search query but between two just OK sites: if yours is the site with a few inbound links via Press Releases, you can often win.

> *The perfect is the enemy of the good (Voltaire).*
>
> *You don't have to run faster than the bear, just faster than your buddy (Unknown).*

To see examples of Press Releases issued by the JM Internet Group with examples of proper link formatting, visit http://jmlinks.com/6q.

» LEVERAGE FREE PRESS RELEASE SYNDICATION SERVICES

Once you've created your press release and uploaded it to your own website, you are ready to leverage press release syndication services. The best **free** service is PRLog.org (http://www.prlog.org/) and the best **paid** service is PRWeb.com (http://www.prweb.com/), owned by Cision. You can learn more about the available packages from Cision at http://jmlinks.com/6s.

If you have budget, I highly recommend setting up a paid Cision account. With a yearly package, the cost per release is about $175. The paid service gets you many times the benefit of the free services like PRLog.org.

After you've set up your account on one of these services, open your press release in one browser window. In another window, log into the press release syndication service and begin the process of submitting a release. Copy and paste the following from your press release into the syndication service -

> **Headline.** Make sure it includes your target keywords!
>
> **Quick Summary**. Write a pithy, exciting one-to-two sentence summary. This will usually become your META DESCRIPTION tag on the syndication service.
>
> **News Body.** Copy and paste your news body. Be sure to embed a URL after the first or second paragraph, and write in the simple *http://* format (since embedded links may not be retained in syndicated press releases).
>
> **URL / Active Link.** Make sure that your press release has at least one prominent link to your website, and **make sure it is in the http:// format**. News is especially good at getting Google to index new web pages on your site!
>
> **Contact Information.** Include a description of your company with a Web link and email address for more information. This is another link-building opportunity.
>
> **Tags.** Select appropriate tags for keyword / content issues as well as target geographies.

Finally, commit to publishing press releases on your website and using news syndication on a regular, consistent basis. It's better to publish one release per month, consistently, than six releases in one month and nothing for six months. For an online press release template, visit http://jmlinks.com/6r.

> **WORKSHEETS.** For the worksheet, go to https://www.jm-seo.org/workbooks (click on "SEO Fitness," enter the code 'fitness2016' to register if you have not already done so), and click on the link to the "press release worksheet."

> **VIDEO.** Watch a quick video tutorial on how to syndicate press releases at http://jmlinks.com/6t.

A Warning about the Penguin Update. Google's latest anti-SEO algorithm update has been called the "Penguin Update." The Penguin Update specifically targets low quality link schemes, meaning many inbound links to your website from low-quality sites that often have the same keyword phrase with a link.

The take-away is to not overdo press release SEO! First, don't issue more than two press releases per month via paid syndication services such as PRWeb.com. Second, to every extent possible, use press releases for "real" news with even the goal of getting "real" people to read them (including journalists) and possibly reach out to your company for more information. Don't issue junk, but then again don't be too modest either.

Post-Penguin the goal is to have a "natural" inbound link footprint consisting of branded, naked, and keyword heavy links. Even a few "click here" links are good to throw into the mix.

» DELIVERABLES: A PRESS RELEASE CALENDAR AND A SAMPLE PRESS RELEASE

The first **DELIVERABLE** for this chapter is your press release calendar. This can be as simple as a Word document or Google document that serves as an "idea list" of when to generate a press release. The goal is to avoid writer's block and get into a rhythm of generating at least two press releases per month. The second **DELIVERABLE** is your first SEO-friendly press release, uploaded to your own site and pushed out via a syndication service such as PRLOG.org or PRWEB.com. Use the "press release worksheet" to guide you to success.

4.3

BLOGGING

Nothing is as easy or as powerful for SEO as blogging! While landing pages reflect your anchor keyword terms, and press releases can build inbound links via syndication, blogging allows you to sculpt content for narrower keyword queries as well as to respond quickly to industry buzz and trends. In addition, frequent blogging - like frequent press releases- sends a powerful signal to Google that your website is "fresh." Every website should have a blog!

Let's get started!

TO DO LIST:

- Make a Blog Calendar
- Set Up Your Blog for Best SEO
- Write SEO-friendly Blog Posts
- Deliverables: Blog Calendar and Your First Blog Post

>> MAKE A BLOG CALENDAR

Today's SEO ecosystem heavily rewards sites that blog on keyword-heavy topics. Blogging without knowing your keywords is an exercise in sheer *vanity*, whereas blogging with keywords in mind is a powerful *tool* to get you to the top of Google. Moreover, your blog can connect to your social media strategy as a "long read" to complement the "short reads" on Twitter, Facebook, or Google+. A good blog post gives you something to "point people to" on social media.

As an SEO Content strategist, look around your company and identify blog topics as well as other company employees who can contribute to the blog. Unlike press releases, blog posts can be much more informal, opinionated and quick. So whereas you might generate just two press releases per month, set a goal of at least one blog post per week, if not more. I generally recommend two press releases per month and four blog posts per month as a solid website goal.

You cannot overblog! As long as your blog content is fresh, original, and keyword-heavy, all blogs posts will help your SEO. The more the merrier!

Depending on your company, a blog calendar can help you keep track of possible blog topics and themes.

Here is a sample blog calendar for a hypothetical roofing company in Dallas, TX.

Sample Blog Topic:	When To Post:
We complete a roofing job.	Write a blog post about each roofing job, when completed, with information on the city where the job was located, the type of roofing material used, and customer reaction. Goal is to help with geotargeted searches.
Our day-to-day in a host city for a job.	Because geographic search terms are important for a roofing company, create city-specific blog posts such as your favorite "taco joint" in the city, or variances in city roofing codes.
Industry trends and events	Any time there is an industry trend, such as a new roofing material, chime in with an opinion. Ditto for any industry events or events in the Dallas, Texas, area.
New website content	Blog about our website, explaining what new content we are creating and why.
Partnership Announcements	Identify potential blog opportunities with our partners.
Industry Awards or Milestones	Any time we win an industry award or cross a milestone (such as the 1000th follower on Twitter), it's time for a blog post!

You'll see many similarities between successful SEO blogging and SEO press releases. The difference is one of degree: blogging is quicker, more informal, and more a quantity play vs. the more formal, higher quality status of press releases.

❯❯ Set up Your Blog for Best SEO

The best blog platform by far is WordPress (http://wordpress.org/). Ask you web designer and/or ISP to install WordPress on your site. If you are building a new site, use an ISP like GoDaddy that makes WordPress a "one click" installation. And, if you don't have the budget for WordPress, I recommend Google's blogger platform at http://www.blogger.com/. Regardless of your platform, follow these basic principles for successful SEO blogging:

> **Host your blog on your own site.** Blogging helps with site freshness vis-a-vis Google as well as acts as link bait. So it makes little sense to host your blog on another site. If at all possible, host your blog at your own domain in the position of http://www.company.com/blog.
>
> **Check each blog post for good SEO.** As you write a blog post, check to make sure that your blogging platform allows for basic "on page" SEO: a keyword heavy TITLE tag, META DESCRIPTION tag, the use of the header family, one image with the alt attribute defined, and keyword-heavy cross-links.
>
> **Make sure your blog allows for keyword heavy tagging and cross-indexing.** Make sure that your blog allows you to "tag" a post with keywords and that these "tags" act as URL cross-links.
>
> **Verify that your blog URLs are keyword heavy.** Numeric, parameter-centric URLs are very bad for SEO, so make sure that your blog generates keyword-heavy URLs for each post.

At the home page level, a best practice is to have "one click" links from your home page down to at least three, rotating blog posts. If you are running WordPress, be sure to install the Yoast SEO plug in (http://yoast.com/).

Many people do not correctly "tag" each blog post, yet tagging is incredibly important to SEO-friendly blogging! Make sure that your blog tags match your keyword themes, and make sure that when you write a blog post each post gets tagged. One of the better blogs to emulate is by Nolo press (http://blog.nolo.com/). Here's a screenshot of the tags at the bottom of the page for a post on bankruptcy forms:

WordPress has two types of tagging: "categories" and "tags." From an SEO perspective, both accomplish the same thing: lumping your posts into SEO-friendly cross-linked URL's. Both are strongly encouraged because both give Google an SEO-friendly URL structure to grab onto. Here's a link to the Nolo blog "bankruptcy" tag: http://bit.ly/nolo-br. Notice how the practitioners at Nolo are churning out blog post after blog post on their keyword theme of bankruptcy and related keywords! And notice the URL structure itself, which mimics the target keywords and signals to Google that this blog has quite a bit of content on bankruptcy:

http://blog.nolo.com/bankruptcy/tag/bankruptcy-2/

» WRITE SEO-FRIENDLY BLOG POSTS

Blogging is a complementary SEO content strategy to your anchor landing pages, your home page, your product pages, and your press releases. Whereas anchor landing pages focus on your evergreen anchor keyword terms, your blog can focus on more keyword specific, timely topics. Blogging is especially useful for posting content that responds to quick industry trends. Here are the steps to writing a good blog post:

1. **Identify the target keywords.** A good blog post is laser focused on a very narrow keyword, so do your keyword research first!
2. **Follow "on page" SEO best practices.** Make sure that your post follows all of the "on page" rules such as a keyword heavy TITLE, META description, etc.
3. **Consider an action or purpose.** Have a defined action for each blog post, usually by embedding a link from the blog post "up to" one of your defined

anchor landing pages. Another use of blog posts such as "Top Ten Things that Can Go Terribly Wrong at Your Wedding" is link bait; people will link to informative, provocative, shocking blog posts.

4. **Tag your blog post.** Identify keyword themes for your blog that match those of your keyword worksheet and recognize that each blog post is part of a keyword cluster, supporting the entire website's SEO themes.

VIDEO. Watch a video tutorial on SEO-friendly blogging posts at http://jmlinks.com/6m.

» DELIVERABLES: A BLOG CALENDAR AND A SAMPLE BLOG POST

The first DELIVERABLE for this chapter is your blog calendar. This can be as simple as a Word document or Google document that serves as an "idea list" of when to generate a blog post. The goal is to avoid writer's block and get into a rhythm of generating at least one blog post per week, if not more. The second DELIVERABLE is your first SEO-friendly blog post, uploaded to your own site and tagged with appropriate (keyword) tags. Use the "page tags worksheet" to step through an SEO-friendly blog post from keyword target to final content.

5.1

LINK BUILDING

Steps #1 to #4 are all "on page" SEO: things you do to your own website. They are todos that you control just as you control the job you want and the resume you build to (hopefully) get a job. In **Step #5**, we cross the Rubicon, shifting our attention to the actions of others through "off page" SEO. *References* matter for a job search, and external *links* matter a great deal for SEO.

Step #5 in the **Seven Steps to SEO Success**, therefore, is to "go social." Google pays incredible attention to how others talk about your website, whether in the format of inbound HTML *links* or inbound *social mentions*. We'll turn first to **links**, the more traditional of the two, and in the next chapter look directly at **social authority** and **social mentions**.

Remember that a link *from* a directory, blog, web portal, or other industry site *to* your website is counted as a **vote** by Google that your site is important. The more links (votes) you have, the higher you show on Google search results for your target keywords. But how do you get links? In this chapter, we outline the basics of effective link building for SEO.

Let's get started!

TO DO LIST:

>> Define Your Link Objectives

>> Beware the Penguin

>> Solicit the Easy Links First

>> Identify Directory, Blog, and Other Link Targets

>> Reverse Engineer Competitors' Links

>> Create Link Bait

>> Deliverable: Link Building Worksheet

>> DEFINE YOUR LINK OBJECTIVES

Just as strong references propel your resume to the top of the heap, strong inbound links from other websites to your site propel your website to the top of Google. At the most basic level, therefore, your objective is to get other websites to link to your website.

Link Basics

What is a link? A link shows up as an underlined blue text phrase (or image) that, when clicked, transports a user FROM another website TO your website. Importantly, it is links FROM other websites TO your website that count for SEO (not the other way round). An easy way to think about links is that links are like "votes," and Google is the vote-counter.

LINKS ARE LIKE VOTES

For example, I want my website (https://www.jasonmcdonald.org/) to rank highly for searches such as "Bay Area SEO Experts." I am an instructor at the Bay Area Video Coalition (http://www.bavc.org/), and on their website's instructor page (https://bavc.org/person/jason-mcdonald) I have a link FROM BAVC.org TO JasonMcDonald.org. Here's a screenshot:

You can view it online at http://jmlinks.com/6u. In addition, I have solicited and nurtured other links FROM other website TO jasonmcdonald.org. You can view a list of sites that link TO JasonMcDonald.org at http://jmlinks.com/6v.

The point is that all of these links are like "votes" to Google that JasonMcDonald.org is an important website, one that should rank highly on Google searches. Another way to think about links is that these links send "energy" or "link juice" to JasonMcDonald.org which propels it to the top.

Link Attributes

Now that you understand what a link is, your first step in link-building, therefore, is to define how you want other people to link to your website. The best links enjoy the following attributes:

- **Good Syntax** - the best links have good syntax with your "keyword / keyphrase" nested inside the <A HREF> tag as in <A HREF="http://www.yoursite.com/">your target keyword</A>
- **Sheer Quantity** - the best links occur in substantial quantities. More is better: all things being equal, the site with more links to it will outrank a site with fewer inbound links.
- **High Authority** (**PageRank**)- the best links come from high *PageRank* websites inside your keyword communities. *PageRank* is Google's determination of a website's authority. A site such as *NYtimes.com* has more PageRank than a site like *TulsaWorld.com*; Google determines their relative authority by the number of links to that site. Essentially, you want "popular" websites to link to your site, thereby making you "popular" yourself. (*Yes, it's a bit circular*).

Most companies have more than one keyword community or "link neighborhood" as it is often called in the SEO industry. If you are a Bed and Breakfast in Boston, Massachusetts, for example, then you "live" in at least two keyword communities: a) Boston, Massachusetts websites, and b) websites in the B&B industry. Use your keyword worksheet to brainstorm the various keyword communities in which you can solicit links.

Remember: it is links FROM other sites TO your site that matter. Links FROM your site TO other sites, have a minimal (at best) impact on your SEO performance.

It's not *who you like* that makes you popular: it's *who likes you*.

A Word about NoFollow

At a technical level, the `rel="nofollow"` attribute tells Google to ignore a link; these types of links are devalued by Google. So if you see *nofollow* in the HTML source code it's a sign that given link is not as valuable. Here's a screenshot from WSJ.com showing a link FROM WSJ.com TO jm-seo.org that includes the nofollow attribute, therefore nullifying the link:

```
regulates Google, technology will probably have moved on.
I teach SEO / Social Media Marketing at <a
href="http://www.jm-seo.org/" rel="nofollow">http://www.jm-
seo.org/</a>.</p>
</div>         </li>        </ul>      </li>     <li
class="commententry    "   >      <a name="comment-385157"></a>
```

You can see it at http://jmlinks.com/6w.

Don't freak out. You don't have to be an HTML source code genius to understand links! Just realize that, generally speaking, links in comments on blogs are all *nofollow*. Craig's list, Wikipedia, and many directories are also *nofollow*. Press release links are commonly *nofollow* too. These links are not as valuable as links that do not have the *nofollow* attribute (called *dofollow* links in SEO lingo).

Do Nofollow Links Matter?

The first take-away is that *nofollow* links do *not* help SEO. This is the official Google position and commonly held position in the SEO community. However (*there's always a however in SEO*), my opinion is that *nofollow* links actually *do* count, and can help your SEO. Think of links like a stock portfolio: you want diversity in your links – some *nofollow*, some *dofollow*, some in the HTTP format, some in your brand name, and some in your keyword syntax. *Nofollow* links are like "penny stocks" – one-by-one, not very valuable but in totality, they can indeed be valuable.

Google, in short, probably devalues the weight of *nofollow* links to the tune of 90% or 95%, but they still seem to carry some weight.

Get Links

Now, before your head is swimming with all this technical mumbo-jumbo: just remember to **get links**. Ask customers, suppliers, and other business contacts whom you know to add a link FROM their website TO your website. It can be as simple as asking the janitorial company that cleans your office, or the pizza company that delivers your office pizza, to go on their website and add a link FROM their site TO your site. Or, to ask a customer who has a blog to write a product review about her experience, and have her include a link in that blog post FROM her blog TO your website.

Register for professional associations that include links to your website. Set up your social profiles on Twitter, Facebook, Google+ and other sites. Ask everyone you know who has a website to write something about your company and link over to it.

Just get links!

Just like in real-world elections, the most important part of successful link building is sheer **quantity**. Politicians don't always sweat the small stuff; they kiss a lot of babies, and shake a lot of hands in their quest for high quality votes. So should you in your quest for links!

POLITICIANS KISS BABIES
SEOs ASK FOR LINKS

▶ BEWARE THE PENGUIN

Google's "Penguin" update, launched in April 2012, is an on-going algorithm attack against artificial link-building. While officially Google says that you should NEVER "build links" but rather just wait "passively" for links to come to your site, a passive strategy will get you nowhere.

You can, must, and should "build links."

However, you have to be aware of Penguin, and solicit links in a smart fashion. First, let's consider what Penguin penalizes, and then let's turn to the "big picture" of link-building, post-Penguin.

First, Penguin penalizes a large quantity of in-bound links from "low quality" websites as well as "overoptimized links." "Low quality" websites are generally artificial blogs – blogs that are poorly written, contain non-related content, and are clearly created "for search engines" and not for people. A good example of this scenario is Indian-based SEO companies that built thousands upon thousands of blogs (called a blog network), and then (for money) will link back to your site around a target keyword phrase such as *Miami divorce attorney,* or *organic baby food.* It is easy for Google to detect this chicanery and penalize sites with this sort of a link footprint.

In fact, if you are solicited by SEO companies offering link schemes that directly involve posting links to your website on low quality blogs or low quality directories, do **NOT** fall for these schemes! They will hurt you much more than help you.

What are Overoptimized Links?

"Overoptimized" links are links from other websites to your website that all include the same keyword phrase over and over. A "divorce attorney," for example, might create / pay for / solicit links from blogs all around the exact phrase "divorce attorney." He would end up with, for example, 1000 blogs all linking back to his website, all having the format of:

> bla, bla, bla, bla, bla divorce attorney (linking to: http://www.divorceattorneywebsite.com) bla bla bla bla bla bla bla

Now, to have 1000 links all exactly alike, all linking back to the same website is "unnatural," isn't it? So what Penguin did was look at the "link footprint" of websites and identify "unnatural" link footprints. It then penalizes these sites by taking them off of Google or harshly pushing them from Page 1 to Page 101.

Penguin looks for "unnatural" link profiles: many links from low quality blogs or directories as well as many optimized links. You can use the Remove 'em tool at http://jmlinks.com/6x to check your own link footprint.

Link Diversity

Second, when building links post-Penguin, you should a) never solicit links from low quality blogs and/or easy, free directories, and certainly not want links from sites the blatantly advertise "links for sale," and b) pay attention to the (over)optimization of your link structure. A good general rule of thumb is 1/3 *http://* links, 1/3 *branded* links (links to your company name), and 1/3 *optimized* links. In HTML code these are written as:

> Check out Jason McDonald's SEO consulting website at **https://www.jasonmcdonald.org/** (naked or http link).
>
> Check out **<a href=http://www.jasonmcdonald.org/>Jason McDonald's</a>** SEO consulting website. (branded link)

```
Check out Jason McDonald, an amazing <a
href=http://www.jasonmcdonald.org/>SEO consultant</a> in
San Francisco. (optimized link)
```

Link diversity means having people link to you in different formats, and to get links from a variety of sources: trade associations, blogs, directories, non-profits, etc.

Fortunately, for most companies, too many links and *too many* overoptimized links are the least of their problems; most companies just have *too few* links. But, that said, if you engage in serious link-building, you must "beware the Penguin" and build a "natural" yet robust inbound link profile. Build links at your own risk!

Outbound Links from Your Website

Finally, Penguin penalizes websites that are "too perfect." Pre-Penguin, many SEO experts would advise you never to link out FROM your website TO other websites. This advice is no longer correct; a website that has zero outbound links looks suspicious to Google. Therefore, post-Penguin, I advise you to strategically link out to highly reputable websites in your industry. A breeder of Brahman cattle, for example, should link out to sites like the National Brahman Association (brahman.org) as well as other websites in the cattle industry. A San Francisco attorney might link to the city of San Francisco (SFgov.org). The objective is to convince Google that you are a good "Net citizen," and you are linking *out* as well as receiving links *in*. Just keep your outbound links to a minimum, and make sure that they are to highly reputable sites in your own industry. Also, I do not recommend the use of the nofollow attribute on your outbound links or on internal links from one web page to another; its use is a clear signal to Google that you understand (too much) SEO.

Let's turn now to what you should be doing pro-actively to attract inbound links to your website, all with an eye to a post-Penguin "natural" link footprint for your website.

» SOLICIT THE EASY LINKS FIRST

Your **ecosystem partners**, i.e. those companies you do business with on a regular basis, are your easiest link targets. If you attend an industry trade show as an exhibitor, for example, ask for a link back to your company website from the trade show website. If you buy a lot of stuff from a supplier, require a link back to your company website from their website as a condition of doing business. If you sponsor a local charity like the *Breast Cancer Walk Pittsburgh*, ask for a link back to your company website from the charity website. If your boss teaches a class at the local university, help him set up a link from his or her profile page back to your company website. If anyone in your company gets interviewed or is able to write a guest blog post on another website, make sure that they get a link back in their author profile!

You get the idea: create a **culture of link solicitation** in your organization, so that on a day-in and day-out level everyone in your company is soliciting links, and (over time) getting them.

Don't forget your **social media profile** links! If local search is important to you, make sure that your company is included in Google+ Local, Yelp, Citysearch and other local listing sites. Be sure to set up a Twitter, Google+, Facebook and other social media profiles for your companies and include links in those profiles. Don't forget your **directory links**! If your industry has serious, quality, industry-specific directories, make sure you are included in those directory listings with links.

Your first TODO is to open up the "link building worksheet," and fill out the easy link target section. For the worksheet, go to https://www.jm-seo.org/workbooks (click on "SEO Fitness," enter the code 'fitness2016' to register if you have not already done so), and click on the link to the "link building worksheet."

» IDENTIFY DIRECTORY, BLOG, AND OTHER LINK TARGETS

Quality directories, blogs, and other websites found on Google make great link targets. How do you find them? For **directories**, do a Google search for keywords such as "AddURL + Your Keywords," "Directory + Your Keywords," and/or "Catalog + Your Keywords." As you browse these sites, make note of their **Web Authority** (*use OpenSiteExplorer.org or AHREFS.com, and the Domain Authority metric*) and **keyword themes** that align with your own target keywords. Use the Solo SEO link search tool (http://bit.ly/link-search) for a quick and easy way to look for possible link targets.

A marriage counselor in Bethesda, Maryland, for example, might search Google for:

> *marriage counselor directory (view this search at http://jmlinks.com/6y)*
>
> *directory of therapists*
>
> *relationship therapist directory*
>
> *directory Maryland businesses*
>
> *directory woman-owned businesses*

Her goals are to a) identify quality directories that have dofollow outbound links, b) figure out how much it costs and/or what are the procedures to be listed, and c) acquire those directory links. **Remember**: if it's absolutely easy to get in, every SEO will do it and the directory will be low quality or contaminated. **You want serious directories that either cost money and/or have real qualifications to be included.** Quality is important!

Identify Relevant Blogs

To find **blogs**, type your target keywords plus the word "blog" into the Google search box. For example, our marriage therapist might type in "marriage therapy blog" at http://jmlinks.com/6z. IceRocket at http://www.icerocket.com/ is a specialized search engine just to find blogs. You're looking for blogs that will allow a guest post and/or blogs that are interested in your keywords. Remember to also pro-actively ask customers if they have a blog, and if they do, solicit them to write something about your company, product or service. Then you have to devise an idea / solicitation that they'd like to include on their blog, plus include a link back to your website.

A common tactic is to give out product samples, for free, in exchange for a product review and link back on the blog.

Complementary Competitors

Finally, do searches for your major keyword phrases. As you search, segregate your **direct competitors** (sites so similar to your own that there is no way that they would link to you) from your **complementary competitors**. These are sites like blogs, personal websites, portals, directories, Wiki entries and the like that "show up" on your searches but may have a complementary reason to link to you. A wedding photographer, for example, might search for not only directories of wedding suppliers but also florists, priests, caterers, bakers, and facilities that would likely exchange links due to the complementary nature of their businesses.

Sponsor Non-Profits and Include Links

Another great tactic is non-profit link-building. Solicit non-profit links: identify relevant non-profits, and pay them as a "sponsor" with a link from their website to your own. As with all link-building tactics, do not overdo this.

A good way to do this is to search Google using the site: command, as in:

    site:*.org "your keywords"

For example: site:*org "organic food" (http://jmlinks.com/7d).

For example: site:*.org "organic food" "link to your website" (http://jmlinks.com/7e).

You thus identify non-profits in your keyword community, and can even drill down to those that allow paying sponsors to link back to their website. Voila: a link-building strategy based on helping non-profits!

Todo for Link-Building

Your second **TODO** is to fill out the section of the "link building worksheet" focusing on blogs, portals, and directories. For the worksheet, go to https://www.jm-seo.org/workbooks (click on "SEO Fitness," and enter the code 'fitness' to register if you have not already done so), and click on the link to the "link building worksheet."

» REVERSE ENGINEER COMPETITORS' LINKS

Wouldn't it be wonderful to be able to "reverse engineer" who links to your competitors, and then solicit links from those websites? You can easily do this.

Many free fabulous tools exist to "reverse engineer" inbound links of competitors. Your objective is to identify complementary websites that link to a competitor but who may also be willing to link to you. Type each competitor's home page URL into these tools, and then surf to the appropriate websites, making note of the PageRank (domain authority), content, and contact information for your "Link Building" target list. Here are my three favorites:

Open Site Explorer by Moz (http://bit.ly/open-explorer). Type your competitor's home page into this tool, or the URL of a highly ranked site on Google. Browse to see who is linking to your competitor.

AHrefs (http://ahrefs.com/). Similar to Open Site Explorer, this free tool allows you to input a competitor URL and reverse engineer who is linking to that competitor.

Open Link Profiler (http://www.openlinkprofiler.org/). This tool tracks new links to your website (or to competitors), and requires no registration and no payment. It's totally free!

Here's a screenshot of Open Site Explorer's analysis of http://www.progressive.com/ showing that that site has over 3600 linking domains totaling to over 13,00 inbound links. No wonder *progressive.com* dominates searches for insurance!

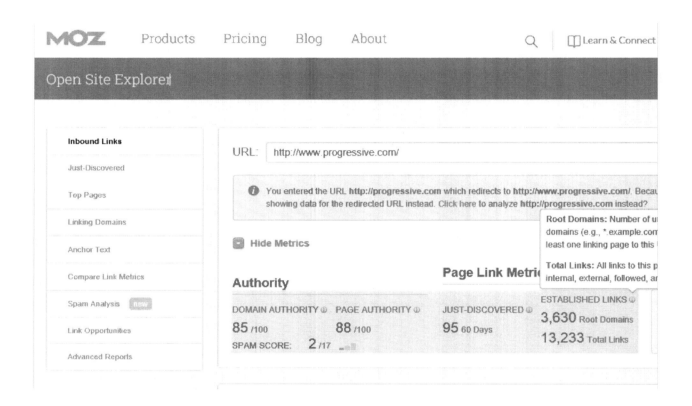

VIDEO. Watch a video review of how to use the Open Site Explorer tool and other link discovery tools at http://jmlinks.com/7a.

At the end of this process, you should have a defined list of "link targets" sorted by PageRank (Domain Authority) and their keyword themes with your "keyword community." Your third TODO is to take this list, and then go one by one through the results, soliciting links from the various targets. If summer is here, link solicitation is a great task for a cheap intern!

» CREATE LINK BAIT

Link bait takes link building to the next level. Link bait is the art of creating content that is so compelling that people will *spontaneously* link to it, without you even having to ask. Let's run through some common link-bait ideas.

Ego Bait

Have a customer of the month contest (if your customers have websites), have a supplier of the month award (if your suppliers have websites). Email, call, and even give gifts to blogs, portals, and other content sites that might be willing to cover you and your company. In link building, remember you are dealing with other people, so look at the situation from their perspective: what's in it for them? If you "feature" them with an award, they'll often spontaneously link to you – plus your "award contest" can get press, publicity, and links.

Product Sample Bait

Give away free samples of your product only to people who have a blog, and/or are willing to share your site on social media. Ask them to write honest product reviews, and require a link back in the blog article.

Scholarship Bait

Identify a noble cause (preferably relating to your keyword targets), and create a scholarship program for deserving students. Next, require an essay as part of the application (which will be great content for your blog, and ego bait). Then, identify relevant colleges and solicit them to link "out" to your scholarship. It's win win: the student gets a scholarship, and you get links from quality .edu domains to your website.

Ultimate Guide Bait

Your **blog** can be great link bait. Write the definitive article on "top ten new technologies" for your industry, write a provocative blot post on why "such-and-such" is a "terrible" idea to stir controversy, share an emotional story. Blog posts that are informative, controversial, or emotional tend to get shared, and linked to, the most.

Here's a great example. PointBlank SEO has written the "definitive guide" to Link Building (which is, in and of itself, link bait) at http://jmlinks.com/7b.

Badge Bait

Consider creating **badges**: customer of the month, best tool for such-and-such, partner companies, verification of a certification test, and so on and so forth.

Have you ever noticed how many Yelp results show up high on Google search? Have you ever thought of how many companies have Yelp badges on their websites, with links up to their Yelp listings? Consider being the "Yelp" of your industry via badges. Here's a screenshot giving an inside look at how Yelp promotes its link juice via badges:

You can view the Yelp badge system at http://jmlinks.com/7f. Note: if you use "badge bait," be Penguin-aware. Make sure to **vary the inbound link text** and structure across your badges so as to not trigger a Penguin penalty. For example, the ALT image attribute for some badges would have keyword No. 1, others keyword No. 1, others just your company name, etc.

Widget Bait

If you have a programming budget, create **widgets** such as BMI calculator, the real-time price of gold, a reverse mortgage calculator. Any sort of free tool or widget that is relevant to your industry can be link bait to bring in links in a spontaneous way. Monex, a company that sells gold, silver, and platinum bullion, for example, has an example of "widget bait" at http://jmlinks.com/7c. **Infographics** are another way to get links: create an informative, humorous, outrageous or shocking infographic and let the links roll in!

Your fourth TODO is to have a company meeting and brainstorm possibilities for link bait. If so, create a step-by-step plan to implement your link bait strategy.

» DELIVERABLE: A COMPLETED LINK-BUILDING WORKSHEET

The **DELIVERABLE** for this chapter is a completed link-building worksheet. For the worksheet, go to https://www.jm-seo.org/workbook (click on "SEO Fitness," and enter the code 'fitness2016' to register if you have not already done so), and click on the link to the "link-building worksheet."

5.2

SOCIAL MEDIA

A topic unto itself, Social Media has many SEO implications. **Social mentions** - that is the sharing of your website links on sites like Twitter, Google+, Facebook and more - is a new kind of **link building**. Having robust **social profiles** (like an active *Twitter feed* or active *Google+ account*) signals Google and its search algorithm that your company is active and important. This is called **social authority**. Indeed, Google+ presents unique SEO opportunities, particularly in the area of having a robust Google+ corporate profile with many local reviews. In addition, Google's partnership with Twitter is a clear sign that having a robust Twitter profile and having your links "tweeted" is now a must-do.

SEO is going social, so in this chapter, we explore the brave new world of **Social Media SEO**.

Let's get started!

TO DO LIST:

- » Understand Social Media SEO
- » Get Social Mentions!
- » Set up Robust Social Profiles
- » Get Google+: Google's Favored Social Network
- » Tweet and Be Tweeted
- » Deliverable: A Completed Social Media SEO Worksheet

» UNDERSTAND SOCIAL MEDIA SEO

Links, as we have seen, count as **votes** in SEO. Google clearly rewards sites that have many keyword-relevant links (especially those from high authority websites), with higher positions on Google search results. Social Media in a sense builds on this network of link authority. How so? While Google has not publically clarified how it uses what are called *social signals* in SEO, we can postulate some logical patterns of how Google might interpret social signals.

> *In a nutshell, having your URL's tweeted, shared on LinkedIn or Facebook, or mentioned on Google+ is a form of link-building.*

Therefore, your todo is to "get tweeted" or "get your URL's shared on Google+, Facebook, and/or LinkedIn."

How does social media impact SEO?

First and foremost, sites that enjoy **inbound links via social mentions of URLs** from social sites like Twitter, Google+, or even Facebook are clearly topical and relevant to Google. A simple *site:twitter.com* search on Google reveals over one billion indexed Tweets, and a simple *site:facebook.com* search on Google reveals over six billion indexed Facebook posts.

Google clearly pays attention to the social sharing of links!

SOCIAL SHARES ARE THE
NEW LINK-BUILDING!

Second, robust and active **social profiles** are another obvious clue to Google of your website's relevance. Many sites link out to their Yelp account, Google+ profile, Twitter account, Facebook page, LinkedIn page, etc., and those social sites can be indexed by Google. Google can clearly "see" how active your company is on social media, how many "followers" you have, and whether those followers, in turn are active and/or important. Most importantly, Google can "count" your "reviews" on Google+, Yelp, YellowPages and other local review sites.

It stands to reason that having an active social media footprint, with active posts, many engaged followers, and many reviews is a new signal to Google about your website's relevance. Indeed, much of this is keyword centric, another reason why knowing your keywords is paramount to SEO success!

Third, social search has made the Web more **human**. Whereas in the past, the creators of Web content were relatively invisible, new ways of communicating "microdata" can tell Google how many reviews your site has, who the content author is, and whether this author has an active, engaged follower community or not. Realizing that SEO is now a **social game** positions your company for not just the present but the future of SEO success on Google.

However, remember that "traditional links" remain far, far more important than social shares to this day: so if you have to choose between a "traditional link" (e.g., from a blog post) and a "social share" (e.g., the Tweeting of your URL), choose the former. **Links still remain the dominant currency of SEO.**

» Get Social Mentions!

Getting **social mentions** of your URLs is a lot like traditional link building. First, look for easy social mention targets. Ask customers, suppliers, and ecosystem partners to tweet your URLs, share your company's blog posts on Facebook, and to "+1" your URLs. Second, "reverse engineer" competitors or use common Google and social media searches to find social media sharers who might be interested in your content.

Get Tweeted

For example, to find people Tweeting on your keywords, go to Twitter advanced search at to , type in your competitor names or your keywords and look for Tweeters who have a) many followers, and b) tweet on your keyword themes. Then reach out to them and encourage them to tweet your latest blog post, press release, or informative new widget. Here's a screenshot showing a search for tweets on "organic food":

Similarly, you can use Buzzsumo (http://www.buzzsumo.com) to identify social shares of your keywords. Here's a screenshot:

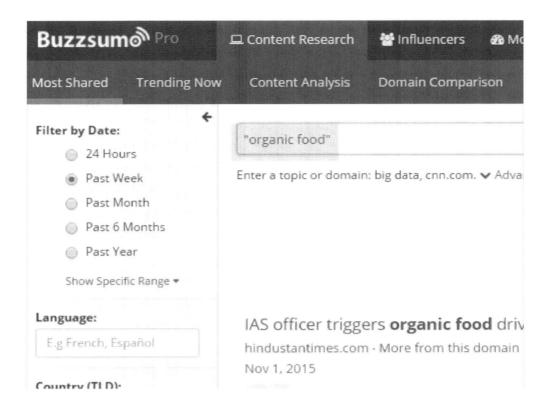

Another good free tool is Topsy (http://www.topsy.com), but unlike Buzzsumo, Topsy only searches Twitter.

Google is another great way to search other social media sites for heavy sharers. Try Google searches like *site:facebook.com {your keywords}*, *site:linkedin.com {your keywords}*, *site:pinterest.com {your keywords}*, etc. to identify site-specific individuals who are good targets to share your own content. You can try a sample search at http://jmlinks.com/7h.

Reach out to Bloggers

Don't forget blogs! Go to Google, type in your keywords plus the word "blog" and look for relevant blogs. Social Mention (http://www.socialmention.com) is another search engine that focuses specifically on blogs, as does IceRocket (http://www.icerocket.com/).

As you reach out for links and social mentions, focus on win-win opportunities. For example, if you sell products send out product samples to key bloggers, Tweeters, and Google+'rs and ask them for honest product reviews in exchange for the samples.

Your first TODO is to open the "Social Media SEO worksheet," and complete the section entitled "social sharers." For the worksheet, go to https://www.jm-seo.org/workbooks

(click on "SEO Fitness," and enter the code 'fitness2016' to register if you have not already done so), and click on the link to the "Social Media SEO worksheet."

►► SET UP ROBUST SOCIAL PROFILES

It's a no-brainer that Google looks for companies with robust social pages. Given two companies competing for a top position on Google, one with thousands of people circling its Google+ corporate page, and another without a Google+ corporate page at all, to whom do you think Google is going to give top placement? This same fact probably goes for other social networks as well, especially ones like Twitter or Pinterest that are open to the Google crawler. (Facebook, unfortunately, is a rather closed system to Google). For each, be sure to fill out your company pages with relevant keywords and cross-link from each social profile to your website. Leaving aside Google+, here are the most important for most companies with links to their business help guides (if available):

Facebook (https://www.facebook.com/business)

Twitter (https://business.twitter.com/)

LinkedIn (http://bit.ly/li-business)

YouTube (http://jmlinks.com/7j)

Pinterest (http://business.pinterest.com/)

Once you set up a business page, be sure to populate your company description with your relevant keywords and cross-link it back to your website. Be sure to also link from your home page to your social network pages to make it easy for Google to see which website corresponds to which social network. All of the networks have easy to use badges that enable these important **cross links**; just look for badges in the relevant business help center as listed above. Be sure to be consistent about your physical address, telephone number, and website address.

Posting SEO-friendly Content

Finally, as you post content to a social network, keep your keywords in minds, grow your fan base, and encourage interactivity between you and your fans. Social media is a two-for-one benefit: first, the *direct* benefit from the social media platform itself as you engage with users, and second, the *indirect* benefit as Google "observes" how popular you are and feeds that data into its SEO algorithm.

Your second **TODO** is to open up the "Social Media SEO worksheet" and complete the section "Social Media Profiles." For the worksheet, go to https://www.jm-seo.org/workbooks (click on "SEO Fitness," and enter the code 'fitness2016' to register if you have not already done so), and click on the link to the "Social Media SEO worksheet."

>> GET GOOGLE+: GOOGLE'S FAVORED SOCIAL NETWORK

Guess who owns Google+? **Google**! Guess who owns search: **Google**!

Think about what that **cross-ownership** means for SEO. Google wants Google+ to succeed, and it "rewards" companies that participate in Google+ with better SEO performance. This is especially true with Google+ local, but it is also true with Google+ (non-Local) business pages and Google+ personal profiles.

GET

GOOGLE+!

Google+ is actually not one but three different social networks:

- **Google+ Profiles.** These are the profiles of individuals on Google+, real people sharing content on Google+ about their lives and favorite websites.

- **Google+ Business Pages.** These are the business pages on Google+, the Fords, Toyotas, and Whole Foods corporate accounts by which businesses promote their wares and connect with customers.

- **Google+ Local Pages.** Now called "Google My Business," these are business pages, similar to those on Yelp, that focus on local search.

And finally there's the Google +1 button (http://www.google.com/+1/button/) (someone "votes" for your website as cool and shares it with his or her friends on Google+) and the Google +1 badge (https://developers.google.com/+/web/badge/), which is a quick way for someone to click from your website to your Google+ corporate account and thereby "circle" you. Get, and enable both of these for your website!

Google+: Not Great Value, But Easy to Set Up

We'll look at Google+ Local in detail in the next chapter, so let's start our examination of Google+ with the **Google+ Business Page** first. This is essentially the same concept as business pages on Facebook. You set up a business page, people "like" you ("circle" you), and thereby when you share messages on Google+, they will see these messages in their news feed on the Google+ social network. From an SEO perspective, being active on Google+ at a business or corporate level probably helps your SEO. It also has a big impact on your branded search terms.

Heretofore, there isn't a lot of real activity on Google+, so I don't recommend spending a lot of time on Google+ for business. Just set it up, enable it, and feed it many of the same posts you're hopefully already doing on Facebook and/or Twitter. You can learn more about Google+ Pages for business at http://bit.ly/biz-gplus.

Next, let's turn to Google+ at an individual level. **Google+ Profile** pages give individuals the opportunity to position themselves as "industry experts." Setting up a Google+ profile for each of your bloggers is, therefore, a must for successful social media SEO. Unfortunately, Google discontinued the use of pictures for Google+ profile participants, but the time and effort to create and populate a Google+ profile is minimal. You can simply post the same content to Twitter and Google+, and be done with it.

In sum, set up both a corporate Google+ page and personal Google+ page(s) for key employee(s), so that Google knows you "love" Google+! The reality is that Google+ hasn't been much of a success, but it's easy to set up and it might have some positive benefit on your SEO – so why not?

» DELIVERABLE: A COMPLETED SOCIAL MEDIA SEO WORKSHEET

The **DELIVERABLE** for this chapter is a completed "Social Media SEO worksheet." For the worksheet, go to http://www.jm-seo.org/workbook (enter the code 'fitness' to register if you have not already done so), and click on the link to the "Social Media SEO worksheet."

5.3

LOCAL SEO

Many Google searches are **local** in nature. Searches like "pizza," "divorce attorney," or even "SEO consultants" tend to have a local nature, and Google is pretty good at inferring which searches have a local character. Users in turn often append geographic terms to their Google searches such as "NYC" or "SF" to clarify to Google that they want "Watch Repair NYC" rather than "Watch Repair Online" and so forth and so on. So if you have a clearly **local** business (*a roofing company, a CPA firm, a watch repair shop, a personal injury law firm, a hypnosis practice...*), **local SEO** is a must.

Even if your business isn't entirely local, local can still be quite relevant. And, local SEO crosses into **review marketing,** an area in which social media and SEO overlap.

Let's get started!

TO DO LIST:

- » Understand Local Search Opportunities
- » Claim and Optimize Your Local Social Media
- » Cross-link Your Website to Your Local Social Media
- » Create a Review Marketing Strategy
- » Identify Reputation Management & Review Opportunities
- » Deliverable: A Local SEO Worksheet

» UNDERSTAND LOCAL SEARCH OPPORTUNITIES

Local search is huge on the Internet. People search for "Dallas Roofer" or "Hypnotherapist New York City" or even just "Sushi." Conduct an inventory of your search keywords and note which queries produce prominent Google+ Local results. Searches for **single** or **short tail** keywords such as "Sushi" or "Divorce Attorney" often produce localized results; take note of which single or short tail searches are especially relevant.

(Google+ Local has now been ignominiously renamed "Google My Business," but I will refer to it as Google+ Local to avoid the nasty tongue-twister of 'Optimize your company's "Google My Business" page).

Second, keep an eye out for other services like Yelp, YP.com, or Citysearch popping up prominently in your local search results. Review your keyword worksheet and designate those searches (usually the short tail searches) that trigger Google+ Local results. You can tell if Google is "going local" because you will see a list of two or more companies with their addresses on the search results page. Here's a screenshot for "Italian Restaurant" with location set to Tulsa, Oklahoma:

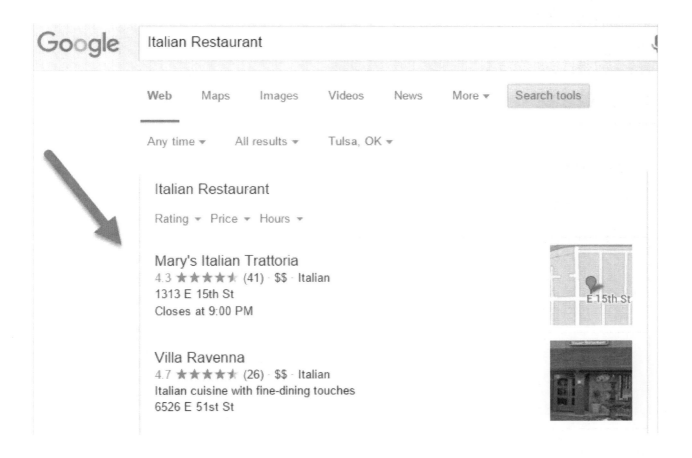

Google makes nearly continuous changes to the format of these results. Currently, the common format is what's called the "Snackpack," three top results in the local listings usually indicated by stars. A few things of note here:

- The more stars a company has, the more likely it is to appear at the top of the three free local listings.
- The stars are driven by reviews exclusively on Google+, despite the fact that few consumers actually use Google+ (*a paradox to which we will return*).
- The format is very similar on the mobile phone, although on the phone, AdWords ads often dramatically crowd down the "free" local listings.
- The local SEO-optimized listings appear below the "snack pack."

Consumer may ignore both the ads and the local Google+ listings and proceed to the organic results below them.

Note, therefore, that sites such as Yelp, Urbansppon, Citysearch, and Yellow pages often appear very prominently on the organic results. This speaks to the fact that if local is important to your business you need an optimized listing on Google+, on Yelp, on YellowPages, etc.

Even for other types of searches, you can still see localized results. With your location set to Tulsa, OK, for example, a search for "SEO companies" brings the following listing to position #5:

> **On First Page SEO - Tulsa OK | Tulsa SEO Company | Tulsa ...**
> www.onfirstpage.com/
> On First Page SEO - Tulsa OK | Tulsa SEO Company | Tulsa SEO Internet Marketing | Affordable Tulsa SEO company. Effective, ethical Tulsa SEO internet ...

Indeed, on the right hand of the screen you may even see a "Knowledge Graph" type box, prominently displaying this local SEO company as follows:

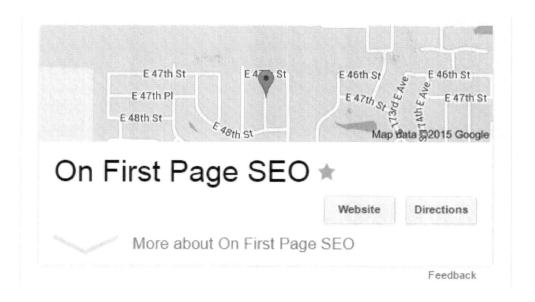

The take-aways here, are:

- If local search matters to your company...
- Some searches may produce the Google+ local "Snackpack," usually consisting of the top three local results.
- Reviews have a huge impact on who shows in the top results, and these are reviews on the Google+ social media network.
- Local results can also appear underneath the "Snackpack," as well as on other types of searches that Google localizes without producing the "Snackpack."

Your first **TODO** is to revisit your keyword worksheet and identify those search queries that generate **local results** on the Google SERP results. This identifies the search patterns for which you really need to focus on local SEO tactics, to which we now turn.

» CLAIM AND OPTIMIZE YOUR LOCAL SOCIAL MEDIA

Your second **TODO** is to claim your local listings. Start with **Google+ Local** (https://www.google.com/business) and follow the instructions to claim your listing there. Be sure to claim your listing with an email address and Google account that is a corporate asset, as it is quite difficult to transfer a Google+ Local listing from one user to another!

VIDEO. Watch a video on how to find your business on Google+ local at http://jmlinks.com/7r.

To begin the process of claiming your business, you can also start at https://google.com/business and follow the instructions there. **Important:** safeguard the email address and password by which you claimed your listing as it is very, very difficult to reset a Google+ local password!

Next, start the process of optimizing your business listing vis-a-vis your target keywords. Essentially, take the keywords from your keyword worksheet and make sure that they appear in your Google+ listing.

Business Description

Once you've claimed your listing, be sure to optimize it by writing a keyword heavy description, for example. Pay attention to the first paragraph, and create an optimized link (keyword) around one of your target keywords, from your Google+ business page to your website. For an example, view the local listing of the JM Internet Group at http://jmlinks.com/7s. Note that this is optimized for the phrases "SEO Company San Jose" and "SEO Companies San Jose" on Google, which you can try at http://jmlinks.com/7t.

Posting Strategy

Next, in terms of social media, Google pays attention not only to the **keyword-optimization** of your business listing but also your **social authority**. First, begin to post to Google+. Admittedly, few "humans" use Google+, so you might post the same content to Google+ that you are posting to Facebook. Or you might just share a few blog posts from your blog. The point is to "be active" so that Google sees that your Google+ social media profile is not only on your keyword themes but also active in terms of posting. If possible, get people to 'follow" you on Google+ to increase your follower count and page views. Do everything humanly possible to look and be active on Google+, as this feeds into whether you show on relevant Google local searches. You'll see, for example, that the JM Internet Group has 20 followers to our local Google+ page, and over 33,000 page views. This, in combination with keyword optimization and over 15 reviews, propels us to the top of localized Google searches such as "San Jose SEO companies."

The Steps to Google+ Local Success

Whether you are a Dallas dog groomer, a New York pizza restaurant, or a Seattle artisan coffeehouse, the steps are the same:

- **Identify** and **claim** your Google+ listing for your local business.
- **Optimize** the listing description and categories with keyword-heavy content as well as links back to your website.
- Begin **posting** to Google+, especially on keyword-relevant topics.
- Get **followers** and **views**.
- Solicit **reviews** from happy customers (more about this below).

Beyond Google+, **find**, **claim,** and **optimize** your other local listings across the major sites. Here's a list of the most important sites for social media at a local level:

Yelp (http://biz.yelp.com/) (No. 2 in importance after Google)

Others (all about the same in importance) –

Citysearch (http://www.citysearch.com/)
Bing Places (https://www.bingplaces.com/)
CitySearch (http://www.insiderpages.com/)

A couple nifty services that help you identify and claim your local listings are at https://moz.com/local and http://www.yext.com/. For free, they'll scan what's out there; for a fee they will help you optimize the second-tier listing services after Google+ and Yelp. Use these tools but remember that Google+ is the market leader.

Pay Attention to Yelp

After Google+ Local, Yelp is No. 2. It has a huge impact on Bing search results, and Yelp often appears high on Google organic search results pages, driving consumers FROM Google TO Yelp. So pay a lot of attention to Yelp.

After Google+ and Yelp, claim and optimize your 2nd tier listings such as Citysearch or YellowPages. I recommend using the Yext service to manage these listings.

» CROSS-LINK YOUR WEBSITE TO YOUR LOCAL SOCIAL MEDIA

Consistent Citations

Once you've successfully claimed your listings, it's time to cross-link your website to your listings, especially Google+ and Yelp. Your third TODO is to cross-link the website to the listing URLs. Your listing on Google+, Yelp, and other local review sites should have a) the **same** address and **telephone number** as on your website, and b) a **link** to your website. This is called a **citation**, and you want citations to be consistent across the Web. It is very, very important to use the same address and same phone number consistently across all the local listing sites as well as your own website. Please do this accurately!

Now, you are doing the reverse: linking from your website to your local listings.

Preferably on your home page, or at least on your "about" or "contact us" pages, add a link from your website to the direct listing address. The local listing URLS can be quite long and you must get them exactly correct. Review the JM Internet Group "about" page and how it cross-links to both Google and Yelp at https://www.jm-seo.org/san-jose-seo/. Be sure that your physical address appears on your website!

By using a consistent name, address, and phone number across your listings and by cross-referencing them to each other, you help Google "see" which website goes with which listings. Make it easy for Google to localize your website, and Google will reward you with better rankings. The same is true for Bing and Yahoo.

▶▶ CREATE A REVIEW MARKETING STRATEGY

Customer reviews matter! The more reviews you have from people in your local community, people who use your target keywords in their reviews, and people who are active reviewers, the more Google will propel your website to the top of its local search results. Reviews are, in fact, a lot like links and Google clearly rewards websites that have more reviews.

GET REVIEWS

FROM HAPPY CUSTOMERS

After claiming and optimizing your local listings, your next TODO is to create a review marketing process. *Encourage* your happy customers to review your business in every way possible - on Google, on Yelp, on Citysearch, and on any other local listing site important to you.

For review marketing:

- Make sure that at the **end of a successful sale**, your customer is politely asked to review you on Google Places, Yelp, Google Merchant Center (Google Shopping), etc. Make "Please review us!" part of your sales process.
- Think of using **real-world promotions** to encourage reviews such as stickers, cards, brochures at your place of business that ask people to "review you" on social media sites.
- Use **follow up emails** with customers as well as social media like Facebook to thank people who have already reviewed you, and to encourage people who might.

Remember that, technically speaking, it is a *violation* of terms of service to solicit paid reviews, so encourage reviews in a judicious and polite manner! Paying for reviews can be dangerous because, if discovered, your site may be removed from Google, Yelp, or another service.

The Review Dilemma

Reviews cross SEO into social media. Here's the problem. All things considered,

- the **MOST LIKELY** person to write a review of your local business is the **UNHAPPY** customer;
- therefore, if you do nothing, you are **LIKELY** to get only **NEGATIVE REVIEWS**; but
- the **OFFICIAL** policy of Google+, Yelp, and other services is "**THOU SHALT NOT SOLICIT REVIEWS**."

Now if you are a restaurant, coffee house, or some other "fun" type of business, this may not be a big problem. People will indeed spontaneously write reviews of restaurants. In that case, you may just need to pro-actively ask happy customers, "Hey, could you do me a favor? Go on Google+ (or Yelp) and write an honest review of your experience. We'd really appreciate it!)."

But... aside from restaurants, bars, and other fun types of businesses... the situation is much more dangerous. Let's take an example: a plumber. Here's the scenario:

> *My toilet overflows. I panic. I call a plumber, after finding him on Google (Google+), and noting he has many positive reviews. He comes out, fixes my toilet, and hands me a bill. He did a good job. I'm relieved as my toilet is fixed! However, I am not overjoyed nor proud (as I would be of getting a table at an exclusive Italian restaurant in San Francisco), so I am UNLIKELY to login to Google+ or Yelp and write a positive review. I am not that excited about my toilet repair!*
>
> *But let's say he doesn't do a good job. Or he overcharges. Or he's grumpy. Or the toilet breaks the next day, and he doesn't come out for free to fix it. I am now mad as hell. I think to myself, "Oh, I'll show you: I am going to go write a bad review about you on Google+, Yelp, etc.).*
>
> *The point, in sum, is that the UNHAPPY customer is much, much more likely to write a review of a plumber than a HAPPY customer.*

What's the solution? You must pro-actively ask HAPPY customers for reviews. Something as simple, as "are you satisfied with the plumbing job? You are... Could you do us a favor: write us a review on Google+, Yelp, etc.) – will often make a huge difference. Secondly, you might reward not the customer but rather your employee. Offer each plumber a $50.00 bonus if/when a review is posted about him and his service. In that way, the employee has an incentive to proactively ask. A service that automates the review-seeking process is ReviewBuzz at http://www.reviewbuzz.com/.

Legal Disclaimer

You are responsible for everything you do in terms of your Internet marketing. Nothing I am writing here should be construed as required or recommended advice. Legally, I am recommending that you do nothing in terms of review solicitation. I am merely pointing out how many companies "solicit reviews."

Take responsibility for your own actions as a marketer, and act on your own risk!

More sophisticated strategies are discussed in my *Social Media Marketing Workbook* in the chapter on "Yelp Local," available on Amazon at http://bit.ly/smmworkbook.

Encouraging **positive** reviews in a judicious manner is a critical part of local SEO, despite official policies of Google+, Yelp, and other review sites.

» IDENTIFY REPUTATION MANAGEMENT AND REVIEW OPPORTUNITIES

Review marketing doesn't apply only in terms of local SEO, however. Be sure to pay attention to your **branded** and **reputational** searches. Examples are:

> *Company name – branded search: Geico, Bank of America*
>
> *Company name plus terms like reviews – reputational search such as "Geico Reviews" or "Reviews of Bank of America."*

Google your branded and reputational searches on a regular basis, and watch out for negative attacks against your company. The best defense against nasty negative press online is to pro-actively optimize the Web with positive brand mentions about your company.

Claim and Optimize Your Social Profiles

Your best step is to claim and SEO-optimize your relevant social media sites (e.g., Facebook, Twitter, LinkedIn, etc.), as well as create a few duplicate websites, if necessary, optimized on your company name and helper words such as *reviews*. In addition, generate press releases and syndicate them via a service like CISION, with your company name and branded terms.

The point here is to use SEO to prophylactically prevent unhappy customers from attacking your brand online. (*Now, of course, do everything you can to have truly happy customers and prevent the "customer from Hell" from arising in the first place*).

Your TODOS in terms of **reputation management** SEO are:

- **Identify your branded terms** (company name) plus your reputational phrases (usually company name plus terms like reviews).

- **Monitor these searches** on Google and Bing.
- Prophylactically, **set up and SEO-optimize your major social profiles** such as Facebook, Twitter, LinkedIn, etc. (even if they have zero social value – you are doing this for the SEO value in terms of reputation management).
- Use **press releases** and **micro websites** to crowd out the top results on Google for your company name and/or reputational searches.

To see this in action, Google "JM Internet Group" (http://jmlinks.com/7u) and "JM Internet Group Reviews" (http://jmlinks.com/7v). Notice how Google is full of all of the social media sites as well as press releases for the company. Now, obviously, we have only happy customers! But the point is that we have SEO-optimized for our branded term and reputational term in advance of any negative attack by an unhappy customer or competitor. Reputation management, in short, is an important task for effective search engine optimization.

» DELIVERABLE: A LOCAL SEO WORKSHEET

The **DELIVERABLE** for this chapter is a completed "Local SEO Worksheet. For the worksheet, go to https://www.jm-seo.org/workbooks (click on "SEO Fitness," and enter the code 'fitness2016' to register if you have not already done so), and click on the link to the "Local SEO Worksheet."

6.1

METRICS

Google Analytics is the best free Web metrics tool available today. It is, however, only a tool: it doesn't tell you what to measure, nor what to do with the information you acquire. Before you even start with Analytics, your first step is to think through *what* you want to measure, and *why* you want to measure it. Common metrics are your rank on Google for target keyword queries, which data queries get traffic to your website, other ways people find your website, and whether landings on your website convert into goals, such as registrations or sales. Second, after you've identified what you want to measure, you need to turn to not just Analytics but other metrics tools and understand how to use them. They're not easy to use! Third, there are even more advanced techniques that can "slice and dice" your data so that you truly know what's going on with your website.

Let's get started!

To Do List:

» Define Your Goals

» Measure Your SERP Rank and Domain Authority

» Use Google Analytics Basic Features

» Use Advanced Features in Google Analytics

» Deliverable: Google Analytics Worksheet

» Deploy Circular Analytics for Improved SEO

» DEFINE YOUR GOALS

Metrics, especially as seen through the prism of Google Analytics, can seem overwhelming. For most companies, there are just three basic things to measure: **rank** on Google, traffic **sources**, and user **behavior**. Only the latter two can be measured via Google Analytics. Here is a breakdown:

1. **Your Rank on Google Searches and Domain Authority.** SEO starts with whether your website is in position 1, 2, or 3 on Google or at least page one. In addition, you should measure your Google PageRank or domain authority over time. Neither of these important variables can be measured in Google Analytics directly. I also recommend tracking the number of **followers** you have on social media (Twitter, Google+, LinkedIn, etc.) and the **number of reviews** you have on local listing services (Google+, Yelp, etc.).
2. **Traffic Sources.** Learn how people *find* your website, especially your best performing keywords and referrer websites.
3. **User Behavior.** Learn what people *do* once they land on your website, especially marketing goals such as registrations or completed sales. Understand *successes* and *failures* and investigate ways to improve the success rate.

When designing your website for effective SEO, I recommend you identify a few concrete **goals**. Typical goals for most website are:

Registration. Getting potential customers to fill out a registration form usually for a "free consultation," "free webinar," or other "free" offer. The object is to get a sales lead (name, email, phone number).

Purchase. Getting potential customers to actually buy a product. This is typical for less expensive products that people might buy direct from your website.

In both cases, after the person completes the "action," they should get a "thank you" form. In Google Analytics, this "thank you" becomes codified as your "goal" and can be measured vs. incoming web traffic, or clicks, as a "conversion."

The measurement process then is:

1. Identify your target SEO **keywords**.

2. Measure whether you **rank** on Google for them, especially in the top three or top ten positions.
3. Use Google Analytics to measure whether you are actually getting **traffic** from the keywords for which your rank.
4. Use Google Analytics to measure what that traffic does on your website (**behavior**), especially when and where it "bounces" off your site, and when it "converts" to your goal.
5. Use this information to constantly **improve** your SEO.

» MEASURE YOUR SERP RANK AND PAGERANK

Your **SERP rank** (Search Engine Results Page) measures your website's position on a target search query. Your **PageRank**, in contrast, is a measurement of your authority on the Web. It is not really publically released, so use third-party tools that will give you your **domain authority**. As we learned in link building, think of your PageRank as a measurement of how important your site is on the Web.

To measure your SERP rank, the best free tool is Rank Checker by SEOBook (http://www.seobook.com/). The tool is available only on Firefox. After installing it, go to Tools > Rank Checker > Options and set the "delay between queries" to 99 seconds. This is because if you run a long keyword list, Google will stop providing rank data to the tool. Then to run the tool from Firefox, go to Tools >Rank Checker > Run > Add Multiple Keywords. Enter your domain and keyword list, hit start and the tool will measure your rank on Google and Bing.

Another great rank measurement tool is from Sitemapdoc.com (http://jmlinks.com/7w). With their tool, you can measure your rank on any query one at a time, instantly. Good paid tools is AHREFS.com or SERPS.com.

Your first TODO is to revisit your **keyword worksheet** and input your rank for target sample phrases. I usually create a tab called "sample keywords" and measure my rank on Google keyword queries before I start an SEO project, after I have implemented the "on page" changes, and every month thereafter. I then look for ranks *greater than ten* as bad, *greater than three* as in trouble and work on those priority keywords.

> **VIDEO.** Watch a video on how to use the Rank Checker tool at http://jmlinks.com/7x.

Link Metrics

Secondarily, I recommend you measure your **domain authority** as a surrogate for Google PageRank on a monthly basis. Go to Open Site Explorer at http://jmlinks.com/7y, input your website home page URL, and note the four metrics at the top of the page: domain authority, root domains, and spam score. Record each of these on your keyword worksheet each month. Here's a screenshot for jm-seo.org:

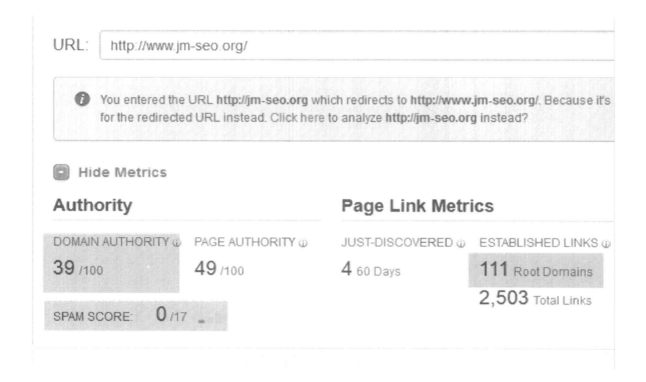

Domain authority is a surrogate for Google PageRank, or a metric that measures how important Google thinks your website is. A site like nytimes.com might be 100, whereas jm-seo.org is a 39, and a tiny, unimportant site might be a 7. What's important is your domain authority relative to competitors, and whether this improves over time. **Root domains** is the number of websites that link to you: again, you want this to grow over time. The **Spam score** is an attempt, after Google's Penguin update, to measure whether your site is on the "naughty list" or not.

Another good site to use for this purpose is AHREFS.com. In any case, you want to measure on a monthly basis your link footprint.

Social Media Metrics

Third, measure your followers on Google+ and Twitter, your page views, and your review count on Yelp and Google+. You want these all to move in a positive direction, over time. Increasingly, SEO is "going social," so it's a good time to be aware of how your social authority is improving over time.

» USE GOOGLE ANALYTICS BASIC FEATURES

Now that you have a measurement of your SERP rank vs. target keywords and your domain authority out of the way it's time to turn to Google Analytics. Google Analytics is a powerful, and free, metrics tool suite available at https://www.google.com/analytics. Log on to create your free account. The first and most important step is to download and install the **Javascript tracking code**. Following the instructions at Google Analytics, and place this code in the <HEAD> tag at the top of *each and every* page on your website. (For a Google tutorial on how to do this, go to http://bit.ly/ga-tracking).

If you are using WordPress, use a good plugin like *Yoast for Google Analytics* at http://jmlinks.com/8e, and it will automatically install the Google tracking code on all your pages.

Once you have installed the Javascript code on your site and allowed enough time to elapse for data to accumulate, it's time for some basic Analytics.

- Click on **Audience**, to see basic data about how many visitors are coming to your website daily, where they are coming from, and basic traffic sources such as search engines vs. referring sites.
- Click on **Acquisition** and browse "referring" sites such as blogs, portals, news releases, etc., that are sending users from their website to yours via clicks.
- Click on **Acquisition, Search Engine Optimization, Queries** to see which keywords and key phrases are performing well for you in generating incoming web traffic. (Link your Google Analytics to your Google Webmaster Tools or Search Console for this feature).
- Click on **Behavior**, **Site Content**, and then **Landing Pages** and **Exit Pages** to see the most popular pages for entering and exiting your website.
- Click on **Conversions**, **Goals**, **Overview** to see whether traffic is "converting," usually buying stuff on eCommerce and/or filling out feedback forms as sales leads.

Basic Analytics provides you a lot of key information on incoming web traffic such as geographic location, mobile platform, and browser version. Finally, you can click on the date field at the top far right of Analytics to change the date filter for data or to compare two time periods.

» USE ADVANCED FEATURES IN GOOGLE ANALYTICS

Beyond Basic Analytics, there are advanced features in Google Analytics that you do not want to miss. First, click on **Advanced Segments** to "slice" and "dice" your data based on criteria such as "new visitors" vs. "repeat visitors" or the geographic locations from which visitors come. Google hides this feature behind the "All Sessions" area when you first login. Simply click on that to bring forth Advanced Segments:

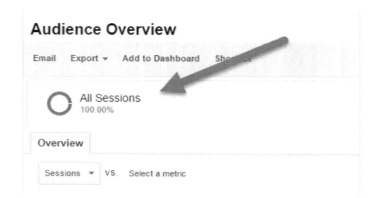

Advanced Segments

You can save any Advanced Segment and use it as a filter throughout Analytics. Set up an Advanced Segment, for example, by geographic area, and then click back to **Traffic Sources** to see which keywords worked better for you in that particular geographic area.

Goals and Conversions

Second, set up "Goals" for Analytics by registering your "Thank you" page after a registration or purchase. To do this, go to the primary log in page on Analytics by click on the "Admin" icon in the top right of the page. Next, click on your profile name (usually your website URL). Then click on "goals" in the middle of the page. Here is where you define a "goal" and a "funnel," which is the steps taken to reach the goal. In

151 | SEO Fitness Workbook

Advanced Analytics, you can therefore see not only how people get to your website but the steps that take as they click through your website.

> **VIDEO.** Watch a video on how to set up goals in Google Analytics at http://jmlinks.com/7z.

Once a goal is set up, you can go back to the main page in Google Analytics, and use Advanced Segments to slice and dice your data and thereby see what traffic is converting (i.e., completing your goal) vs. what is not.

Help is available at the top left corner under the "gear" icon. Here's a screenshot:

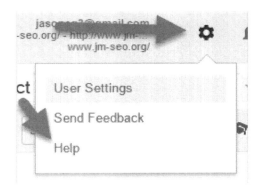

Finally, don't miss some of the free official Google videos available for learning more about Analytics. These are located at the **Google Analytics Academy** at http://jmlinks.com/8a. Ironically, these Analytics IQ Lessons are nearly impossible to find or get to from inside of Google Analytics. (They're hidden behind the graduation cap. Here's a screenshot:)

That's Google for you!

▶▶ DELIVERABLE: GOOGLE ANALYTICS WORKSHEET

The **DELIVERABLE** for this chapter is a completed Google Analytics worksheet. For the worksheet, go to https://www.jm-seo.org/workbooks (click on "SEO Fitness," and enter the code 'fitness2016' to register if you have not already done so), and click on the link to the "Google Analytics worksheet."

▶▶ DEPLOY CIRCULAR ANALYTICS FOR IMPROVED SEO

Analytics coupled with rank measurement gives you powerful data about how you stand on Google for your target keywords, what keywords work for you in generating incoming clicks, and what people do on your website once they arrive. As with a physical fitness program, your metrics objective is to measure **before**, **during**, and **after** your SEO efforts.

Google calls this "circular analytics," whereby you measure not only how people get to your website but how they "convert" into Goals. Then you theorize new changes to your website such as new landing pages, new structural arrangements to content and text, new offers such as "free consultations" or "free events," and measure your success rate vs. your bounce rate. Your goal with circular analytics is to improve your SEO by a constant process of experimentation and measurement. In SEO, as in all things, success takes constant effort!

Good luck!

7.1

LEARNING

SEO is a competitive game that never stops evolving! The Google algorithm changes and adjusts, user behavior evolves, and your competitors also improve their SEO skills. Recently, for example, social media has become ever more important to SEO, as have both localization and personalization issues. In 2014, Google discontinued authorship for search results, and Panda and Penguin continue to evolve. New algorithm changes are no doubt in the works over at the Googleplex.

All require the successful practitioner of SEO to adapt.

"Never stop learning" must be your motto! In this chapter, I point to resources to help you be a life-long learner.

Let's get started!

To Do List:

» Download the Free Companion *SEO Toolbook*

» Use the Worksheets

» Bookmark and Read SEO Media Resources

» A Final Request: Please Review me on Amazon

» DOWNLOAD THE FREE COMPANION TOOLBOOK

The *SEO Toolbook* is a companion to this *SEO Workbook* and contains hundreds of free tools, organized by the Seven Steps. Register for **free** materials, including my SEO Toolbook, SEO Dashboard, and companion worksheets to this book at https://www.jm-seo.org/workbooks/. Click on "SEO Fitness," and enter the password **fitness2016** when prompted.

» USE THE WORKSHEETS, RESOURCES, AND QUIZZES

Throughout this *SEO Workbook*, I have referenced helpful worksheets, videos, and resources. These follow the Seven Steps methodology and can be accessed at the book landing page after you have registered.

» BOOKMARK AND READ SEO MEDIA RESOURCES

SEO changes frequently, so I urge you to pay attention to Google directly as well as the many wonderful blogs that cover search engine optimization. Those are available in the *SEO Toolbook*.

In addition to the companion *SEO Toolbook*, I produce a free **SEO Dashboard**, listing the top, free learning resources for staying up-to-date on SEO. Among the best blogs, I recommend Danny Sullivan's Search Engine Land (http://searchengineland.com/) in particular as well as their conference called SMX (http://searchmarketingexpo.com/). I also recommend checking Amazon for new books on SEO; don't take my word for it – pay attention to what other experts and gurus say about search engine optimization. Here's a direct link to Amazon's SEO bestseller list: http://bit.ly/seo-books.

NEVER STOP LEARNING

If you have any problems, questions, comments, or just want to talk about life and SEO, please email me at info@jm-seo.org or call 800-298-4065 for help. Good luck!

» A FINAL REQUEST: PLEASE REVIEW ME ON AMAZON

If you've read this far, I want to extend my profound thanks. It's a true labor of love to write any book, and this book has been no exception. If you have a spare moment and the spirit moves you, I would really appreciate an honest review about the *SEO Fitness Workbook* on Amazon. Simply logon to your Amazon account and write your review.

- Here's a link directly to the book on Amazon: http://jmlinks.com/seotoolbook.

When you've done so, please send me a quick email. I have many ways to say "thank you" to my fans – such as review copies of my newest books, quick, free consultations on your website, or just plain old good karma. Thanks in advance for your support.

Printed in Poland
by Amazon Fulfillment
Poland Sp. z o.o., Wrocław